Anonymous

Miscellanies - Moral and Instructive

In Prose and Verse

Anonymous

Miscellanies - Moral and Instructive
In Prose and Verse

ISBN/EAN: 9783744685962

Printed in Europe, USA, Canada, Australia, Japan

Cover: Foto ©Thomas Meinert / pixelio.de

More available books at **www.hansebooks.com**

MISCELLANIES,

MORAL AND INSTRUCTIVE,

IN

PROSE and VERSE;

COLLECTED FROM

VARIOUS AUTHORS,

FOR THE

USE OF SCHOOLS,

AND

IMPROVEMENT

OF

YOUNG PERSONS OF BOTH SEXES.

—◦◦◦◦◦◦◦◦◦◦◦◦—

" 'Tis Education forms the common Mind ;
" Juſt as the Twig is bent, the Tree's inclin'd." POPE.

PHILADELPHIA:

Printed by JOSEPH JAMES, in Chefnut-Street,
between Front and Second-Streets.
M.DCC.LXXX.VII.

PREFACE.

THE right education of youth, being a point of great importance to the present and succeeding generations, it is to be regretted, that the want of proper books for the use of schools, should have been so general a subject of complaint ; and that very few attempts have been made to supply this deficiency by introducing something on such a plan, as might, besid improving the understandings and morals, instructively ar the vacant hours of young people, and have a tendency to der the task of teaching a more agreeable employment.

WITH a view to these objects, the following Miscellanec Compilation is now offered to the public. Most of the extrad which compose it, were collected some years ago, from a va riety of authors, by a person who had no other intention, a the time, but that of preserving them for her own perusal and amusement ; and who, from motives wholly disinterested, has lately, at the request of her friends, consented to their publication, with a hope, that if they are favourably received, it may prove an incitement to some person of greater abilities, to pursue this or a better plan, whereby our schools may be furnished with a book more deserving their acceptance.

IT gives some concern to the compiler, that she neglected to distinguish the different parts, with the names of their authors, at the time they were selected, as it is not now in her power to supply the omission.

THE

THE editor has thought it necessary to remark, that a few verbal alterations have been made in some of the extracts, the better to adapt them to the use of the present design ; but as the sentiments and tenor of the original pieces are not thereby materially changed, it is hoped this freedom will be excused by their respective authors, to whom not the least injury or offence has been intended.

THE EDITOR.

ONE of the most approved judges of books amongst us, after perusing some parts of the manuscript, has expressed his approbation thereof as follows : ·

" I HAVE read, with much pleasure, the manuscript specimen communicated to me of the Miscellanies in Prose and Verse. I am glad to hear they are now ordered for the press.

" A BOOK, containing so many well chosen sentiments, and excellent instructions, put into the hands of our children, " cannot but be highly useful to the rising generation.

B. FRANKLIN."

A MORNING

A MORNING HYMN.

To thee, let my firft offerings rife,
    Whofe fun creates the day,
Swift as his glad'ning influence flies,
    And fpotlefs as his ray.
What numbers with heart-piercing fighs
    Have paft this tedious night !
What numbers too have clos'd their eyes,
    No more to fee the light !
Sound was my fleep, my dreams were gay,
    How fhort fuch time review'd !
My night ftole unperceiv'd away ;
    I'm like the day renew'd.
This day thy fav'ring hand be nigh,
    So oft vouchfaf'd before ;
Still may it lead, protect, fupply,
    And I that hand adore.
If blifs thy Providence impart,
    For which refign'd I pray,
Give me to feel the grateful heart,
    And without guilt be gay.
Affliction, fhould thy love intend,
    As vice or folly's cure,
Patient to gain that gracious end,
    May I the means endure.
Thus from my fix'd or varying fate,
    Some virtue let me gain,
That Heaven, nor high, nor low eftate,
    When fent, may fend in vain.
Be this, and ev'ry future day
    Still wifer than the paft,
That life's improvement to furvey
    May well fuftain my laft.

THE

THE duties of religion, sincerely and regularly performed, will always be sufficient to exalt the meanest, and to exercise the highest understanding. That mind will never be vacant, which is frequently recalled by stated duties to meditations on eternal interests; nor can any hour be long, which is spent in obtaining some new qualification for celestial happiness.

TO love an enemy, is the distinguishing characteristic of a religion, which is not of man but of God. It could be delivered as a precept, only by him who lived and died to establish it by his example.

IF thou dost good to man, as an evidence of thy love to God, thy virtue will be exalted from moral to divine; and that happiness, which is the foretaste of paradise, will be thy reward upon earth.

RECREATION after business is allowable; but he that follows his pleasure instead of his business, shall in a little time have no business to follow.

RESIGNATION.

THOU Pow'r Supreme, by whose command I live,
The grateful tribute of my praise receive;
To thy indulgence, I my being owe,
And all the joys which from that being flow.
Scarce eighteen suns have form'd the rolling year,
And run their destin'd courses round the sphere,
Since thou my undistinguish'd form survey'd,
Among the lifeless heaps of matter laid,
Thy skill my elemental clay refin'd,
The straggling parts in beauteous order join'd;
With perfect symmetry compos'd the whole,
And stampt thy sacred image on my soul;
A soul, susceptible of endless joy!
Whose frame, nor force, nor time, can e'er destroy,
But shall subsist, when nature claims my breath,
And bid defiance to the power of death,

The

'To realms of blifs, with active freedom foar,
And live when earth and hell fhall be no more.
Indulgent God, in vain my tongue affays,
For this immortal gift, to fpeak thy praife.
How fhall my heart, its grateful fenfe reveal,
When all the energy of words muft fail?
Oh! may its influence in my life appear,
And every action, prove my thanks fincere.
Grant me, great God! a heart to thee inclin'd,
Increafe my faith, and rectify my mind;
Teach me betimes to tread thy facred ways,
And to thy fervice confecrate my days;
Still as thro' life's uncertain maze I ftray,
Be thou the guiding-ftar to mark my way;
Conduct the fteps of my unguarded youth,
And point their motions to the paths of truth;
Protect me by thy providential care,
And teach my foul t' avoid the tempter's fnare;
Thro' all the various fcenes of human life,
In calms of eafe, or bluftering ftorms of ftrife,
Thro' every turn of this inconftant ftate,
Preferve my temper, equal and fedate;
Give me a mind that bravely does defpife,
The low defigns of artifice and lies;
Be my religion, fuch as taught by thee,
Alike from pride and fuperftition free;
Inform my judgment, rectify my will,
Confirm my reafon, and my paffions ftill;
To gain thy favour be my only end,
And to that fcope may every action tend;
Amidft the pleafures of a profp'rous ftate,
Whofe flatt'ring charms too oft the mind elate,
Still may I think to whom thefe joys I owe,
And blefs the bounteous hand from whence they flow;
Or if an adverfe fortune be my fhare,
Let not its terrors tempt me to defpair,
But bravely arm'd, a fteady faith maintain,
And own all beft which thy decrees ordain;
On thy Almighty Providence depend,
The beft protector and the fureft friend:

Thus

Thus on life's stage may I my part maintain,
And at my exit thy applauses gain ;
When thy pale herald summons me away,
Support me in that great cataftrophe ;
In that laft conflict guard me from alarms,
And take my foul, expiring, to thy arms.

"BLESSED are the poor in fpirit, for their's is the king-
"dom of Heaven."—Thus our bleffed Saviour opened his fer-
mon on the mount ; and from his example we may be affured,
that humility is the richeft garment that the foul can wear.   By
this word is to be underftood, not an abject poornefs of fpirit,
that would ftoop to do a mean thing ; but fuch au humble fenfe
of human nature, as fets the heart and affections right towards
God, and gives us every temper that is tender and affectionate
towards our fellow creatures.   This is the foil of all virtues,
where every thing that is good and lovely grows.

DESPISE not labour; if you do not want it for food, you
may for phyfic : It ftrengthens the body, invigorates the mind,
and prevents the ill confequences of idlenefs.

OBSERVE the ant, for fhe inftructs the man,
And preaches labour, gath'ring all fhe can,
Then brings it to increafe her heap at home,
Againft the winter which fhe knows will come ;
And when that comes fhe creeps abroad no more,
But lies at home and feafts upon her ftore.

AN EVENING REFLECTION.

WHILE night, in folemn fhade, invefts the pole,
And calm reflection fooths the penfive foul;
While reafon, undifturb'd, afferts her fway,
And life's deceitful colours fade away—

To

To thee, all-confcious Prefence! I devote
This peaceful interval of fober thought.
Here all my better faculties confine,
And be this hour of facred filence thine.
If by the day's illufive fcenes mifled,
My erring foul from virtue's path has ftray'd,
Snar'd by example or by paffion warm'd,
Some falfe delight my giddy fenfe has charm'd;
My calmer thoughts the wretched choice reprove,
And my beft hopes are center'd in thy love.
Depriv'd of this, can life one joy afford!
Its utmoft boaft, a vain, unmeaning word.

But, ah! how oft my lawlefs paffions rove,
And break thofe awful precepts I approve!
Purfue the fatal impulfe I abhor,
And violate the virtue I adore!
Oft when thy better Spirit's guardian care,
Warn'd my fond foul to fhun the tempting fnare,
My ftubborn will his gentle aid repreft,
And check'd the rifing goodnefs in my breaft;
Mad with vain hopes, or urg'd by falfe defires,
Still'd his foft voice and quench'd his facred fires.
With grief oppreft, and proftrate in the duft,
Should'ft thou condemn, I own the fentence juft.
But, oh! thy fofter titles let me claim,
And plead my caufe by mercy's gentle name—
Mercy, that wipes the penitential tear,
And diffipates the horror of defpair;
From rig'rous juftice fteals the vengeful hour,
Softens the dreadful attribute of pow'r,
Difarms the wrath of an offended God,
And feals my pardon in a Saviour's blood.
All-pow'rful grace, exert thy gentle fway,
And teach my rebel paffions to obey,
Left lurking folly, with infidious art,
Regain my volatile, inconftant heart;
Shall every high refolve devotion frames,
Be only lifelefs founds and fpecious names?
Oh! rather while thy hopes and fears controul,
In this ftill hour, each motion of my foul,

Secure

Secure its fafety by a fudden doom,
And be the foft retreat of fleep my tomb;
Caïm let me flumber in that dark repofe,
'Till the laft morn its orient beam difclofe;
Then when the great archangel's potent found
Shall echo 'thro' creation's ample round,
Wak'd from the fleep of death, with joy furvey
The op'ning fplendors of eternal day.

PRIDE hides a man's faults from himfelf, and magnifies them to others.

" THERE is nothing (fays Plato) fo delightful, as the hear-
" ing or the fpeaking of truth." For this reafon, there is no converfation fo agreeable, as that of the man of integrity, who
hears without any intention to betray, and fpeaks without any
intention to deceive.
    Truth is always confiftent with itfelf, and needs nothing
to help it out; it is always near at hand, and fits upon our lips,
and is ready to drop out before we are aware: Whereas a lie
is troublefome, and fets a man's invention on the rack, and one
trick needs a great many more of the fame kind to make it good.

MORAL virtues themfelves, without religion, are but
cold, lifelefs and infipid: It is religion only which opens the
mind to great conceptions, fills it with the moft fublime ideas,
and warms the foul more than fenfual pleafures.

BY reading we enjoy the dead, by converfation, the living,
and by contemplation, ourfelves. Reading enriches the memory, converfation polifhes the wit, and contemplation improves the judgment.

THE commands of Heaven (in the obfervance of which religion principally confifts) are very plain and obvious to the
meaneft underftanding, and are nothing elfe but exhortations to
love and directions for focial happinefs.

GREAT

GREAT is the steadiness of soul and thought,
By reason bred, and by religion taught:
Which like a rock amidst the stormy waves,
Unmov'd remains, and all affliction braves.

WISDOM.'s an evenness of mind and soul,
A steady temper which no cares controul;
No passions ruffle, no desires inflame;
Still constant to itself, and still the same.

ACCOMPLISHMENTS by Heaven were first design'd,
Less to adorn, than to amend the mind;
Each should contribute to this gen'ral end,
And all to virtue as their centre tend;
Th' acquirements which our best esteem invite,
Should not project, but soften, mix, unite,
In glaring light not strongly be display'd,
But sweetly lost, and melted into shade.

AS the gay flowers which nature yields
So various on the vernal fields,
Delight the fancy more than those
The garden gives to view in equal rows;
As the pure stream, whose mazy train,
The prattling pebbles check in vain,
Gives native pleasure, while it leads
Its random waters swiftly thro' the meads;
As birds on boughs, in early spring,
Their wood-notes-wild near rivers sing,
Grateful their warbling strains repeat,
And soothe the ear irregularly sweet;
So simple dress and native grace,
Will best become the lovely face;
For the judicious man suspects
In artful ornaments conceal'd defects.

- - - - ◇◇◇◇◇◇◇ - - - -

MOST of the miseries of life, undoubtedly result from
our straying from the path which leads to content.
FRIEND-

FRIENDSHIP delights in equal fellowſhip,
Where purity of rank, and mutual offices,
Engage both ſides alike, and keep the balance ev'n.
'Tis irkſome to a gen'rous, grateful heart,
To be oppreſs'd beneath a load of favours,
Still to receive and run in debt with friendſhip,
Without the power of paying ſomething back.

NEVER ſay any thing directly tending to your own
praiſe : and when you have done or ſaid any thing that deſerves
it, receive it from others with indifference. Be neither too co-
vetous of it, nor appear diſpleaſed or confuſed at receiving it ;
but when you have done any thing worthy of praiſe, ſuffer
yourſelf to be told of it, without rebuffing thoſe who are doing
you juſtice. In your private thoughts diveſt yourſelf of it,
and return it to God, as the giver of the gift, and the bleſſer of
the action. Give him unfeigned thanks, for making you an
inſtrument of his glory for the benefit of others.

THE advice of Pythagoras is, that as the body is no
more than the ſervant of the ſoul, it ſhould only be nouriſhed
ſo as it may beſt perform an humble and obedient ſervice to it.

THE duties that are owing to friends, are integrity,
love, counſel and aſſiſtance. It is not intimacy and frequency
of converſation, that makes a friend, but a diſintereſted ob-
ſervance of theſe duties.

THERE is no manner of life ſo ſtrait, or miſerable,
that hath not ſome ſolace and conſolation. Jonah had leiſure
to make his prayer unto God, even in the belly of the whale,
and was heard.

IT is ſome ſhort refreſhment to friends and relations, to ſee
and hear from one another, but it paſſeth away ; and we have
here no continuing city, no abiding delights in this world ; our
reſt remains elſewhere. Thoſe we have, loſe much of their
ſweetneſs, from the thoughts of parting with them, even while
we enjoy them ; but the happineſs to come is eternal. BE

BE very careful in your promises, and just in your performances, and remember it is better to do, and not promise, than to promise, and not perform.

NEVER do any thing for your friends, that is not consonant to your honour and your conscience ; you ought always to prefer those to your friends.

————————WITH stealing foot,
Time follows mortals ; overtakes the swift ;
Stops the career of youth, and clogs the wheels
Of trembling age ; and to one common doom
Brings kings and peasants, conquerors and slaves.

RELIGION's force divine is best display'd
In deep desertion of all human aid ;
To succour in extremes is her delight,
And chear the heart, when terror strikes the sight ;
We, disbelieving our own senses, gaze,
And wonder what a mortal's heart can raise,
To triumph o'er misfortunes, smile in grief,
And comfort those, who come to bring relief :
We gaze, and as we gaze, wealth, fame decay,
And all the world's vain glories fade away.

WE need not travel, seeking ways to bliss,
He that desires contentment cannot miss ;
No garden-walls this precious flow'r embrace,
It common grows in ev'ry desart place.

THE varying seasons ev'ry virtuous soul
With various pleasures, in their changes bless ;
Raise chearful hopes, and anxious fears controul,
And form a paradise of inward peace.

WHEN constant faith, and holy hope shall die,
One lost in certainty, and one in joy ;
Then thou, more happy pow'r, fair charity,
Triumphant sister, greatest of the three,

B

Thy

Thy office and thy nature still the same,
Lasting thy lamp, and unconsum'd thy flame,
Shalt still survive—
Shalt stand before the throne of Heaven confest,
Forever blessing, and forever blest. · ·

DEATH seems to enter a cottage only as a gentle deliverer from the miseries of human life; but into courts and the seats of grandeur, with insult and terror. · To languish under a gilded canopy, to expire on soft and downy pillows, and give up the ghost in state, has a more gloomy aspect, than at the call of nature, to expire on a grassy turf, and resign the breathless clay, back to its proper element. What does a crowd of friends or flatterers signify in that important hour, to the most glorious mortal? Which of his numerous attendants would stand the arrest of death, descend into the silent prison of the grave for him, or answer the summons of the supreme tribunal?

BEAUTY is a short-lived flower, which is easily withered: A cultivated mind is a treasure, which encreases every moment; ·at is a rich soil, which brings forth an hundred fold.

A PERSON never appears so ridiculous by the qualities he has, as by those he affects to have. He gains more by being contented to be seen as he is, than by attempting to appear what he is not.

TRUE greatness of soul pays itself, as it were, with its own hands, by the satisfaction of doing good. · ·

PEOPLE may talk like good Christians at their ease; but pretty sentences, and formal speeches, are very trifling remedies to a real and unaffected sorrow.

THAT little incendiary, called the tongue, is more venomous than a poisoned arrow; and more killing than a two-edged sword.

HOW

H O W few there are, that can be freely kind,
Or know to fix their favours on the mind ;
Hence fome, whene'er they would oblige, offend,
And while they make the fortune, lofe the friend.

KNOW that wherever love and virtue guide,
They lead us to the ftate of Heav'nly blifs,
   Where joys unknown to guilt and fhame prefide,
And pleafures, unallay'd, each hour encreafe.

T H E princely pine, on hills exalted,
Whofe lofty branches cleave the fky,
   By winds long-brav'd at laft affaulted,
Is head-long whirl'd in duft to lie ;
   Whilft the mild rofe, more fafely growing
Low in its unafpiring vale,
   Amidft retirement's fhelter blowing,
Exchanges fweets with every gale.

IMITATION of the 126th PSALM.

1

WHEN God reveal'd his gracious name,
   And chang'd my mournful ftate,
My rapture feem'd a pleafing dream,
   The grace appear'd fo great.

2

The world beheld the glorious change,
   And did thine hand confefs ;
My tongue broke out in unknown ftrains,
   And fung furprizing grace.

3

Great is the work, my neighbours cry'd,
   And own'd the pow'r divine ;
Great is the work, my heart reply'd,
   And be the glory thine !

The

4
The Lord can change the darkeſt ſkies,
    Can give us day for night ;
Make floods of ſacred ſorrow riſe
    To rivers of delight.

5
Let thoſe that ſow in ſadneſs wait,
    'Till the fair harveſt come ;
They ſhall confeſs their ſheaves are great,
    And ſhout the bleſſings home.

A MIND formed upon the principles of the goſpel, may look down with contempt upon the luſtre of a throne, and yet know the value, and feel a ſenſe of gratitude, in the poſſeſſion of a crumb. The moſt exalted ſituation in the preſent life is expoſed; yea, probably moſt expoſed, to the faſcinating allurements of temptation; and whoſoever ſhall look heedfully upon thoſe who are eminent for their riches, will not think their condition ſuch as that he ſhould hazard his quiet, and much leſs his virtue, to obtain it. The rich and the poor have their hours of ſorrow, and their intervals of joy; neither poverty nor wealth exempt them from feeling the common calamities of life, nor confer that happineſs we ſo eagerly purſue, but which we muſt not experience, till our race is finiſhed, and our work done.

WHAT in this life, which ſoon muſt end,
Can all our vain deſigns intend ?
From ſhore to ſhore why ſhould we run,
Where none his tireſome ſelf can ſhun ?
For baneful care will ſtill prevail,
And overtake us under ſail :
'Twill dodge the great man's train behind,
Cutrun the doe, outfly the wind.

                                        INDUSTRY

INDUSTRY is needful in every condition of life; we cannot, without it, act in any state to the benefit or satisfaction of others, or to our own advantage and comfort; it is requisite for procuring ease and satisfaction to the mind; and if attended with a good conscience, sweetens our enjoyments, and seasons our attainments; and is a guard to innocence, and a bar to temptation.

A PERSON under the influence and temper of the gospel, will say with gratitude and joy, " I have learned, in whatsoever state I am, therewith to be content." In the most trying circumstances, I have a sure and certain promise, that my bread shall be given, and my water shall be sure; and if I am not favoured with all the elegancies of life, yet I am confident that the God whom I serve, will afford me such temporary supplies, as shall be most conducive to my own happiness and his glory.

TRUE religion will shew its influence in every part of our conduct; it is like the sap of a living tree, which penetrates to the most distant boughs.

ACTION keeps the soul in constant health, but idleness corrupts and rusts the mind; for a man of great abilities may by negligence and idleness become so useless as to be an incumbrance to society and a burthen to himself.

HE is the most worthy of possessing riches, who knows best how to do without them.

KEEP no company with a man who is given to detraction; to hear him patiently, is to partake of his guilt, and prompt him to a continuance in that vice which all good men shun him for.

THOU shalt not curse the deaf, Lev. xix. 14. Those that are absent are deaf; they cannot right themselves, and therefore say no ill of them.

HAPPY are those who can see the beauty of virtue!—Is it possible to see her, without loving her? Is it possible to love her, without being happy?   B 2   Seeking

Seeking for HAPPINESS.

NOT all that parent earth can give,
Can make her children ever live ;
Nor yet afford them happiness—
For creatures ne'er can truly bless.

   If what we drink, and what we eat,
Can never make our bliss complete—
To rich variety of food,
And gay attire, and ev'ry good,
Give honour, titles, pomp and fame,
With ev'ry blessing we can name ;
Give pleasure, profit, knowledge, ease,
Whatever can instruct or please ;
Authority—a vast estate,
With all that maketh rich and great ;
Yet these could never constitute
A man much happier than a brute :
For while our wretched passions reign,
Felicity is sought in vain.

   Where then shall happiness be found ?
That lovely, pleasing, joyous sound.
Great source of bliss ! vouchsafe to shew,
How I this pearl of price may know.

   If grateful souls—if souls resign'd
To thy blest will, this treasure find,
To me, great God ! do thou impart,
A thankful and contented heart ;
Drive far away all diffidence,
And give me, Lord ! true confidence, }
In thy unerring Providence.
Let all my vices be subdu'd,
Replace them, Lord, with gratitude !
My every want do thou redress,
Give me, oh give me, happiness !

----◦---◦--◦◦◦◦◦◦◦◦◦◦◦◦◦◦--◦---◦--◦----

RELIGION, the balm of life, the anchor of hope, the
dispeller of fears, the haven of rest, will carry us into the arms
of him, who is mighty to save from every trouble ; defended
by

by his shield, tho' afflictions spring not out of the dust, they shall
not hurt us; supported by his power, tho' the mighty rage,
they shall not prevail against us; guided by his wisdom, tho'
snares and evils encompass our paths, we shall escape them all.
In vain may be our toil for riches to secure us; but our trust in
him will never be in vain. The arrows of affliction may reach
the very pinnacle of greatness, and cares and terrors climb up to
us, how ever high we may place ourselves; but he is a tower of
defence, a place of safety, a rock of salvation. O then!
amidst all the storms, and tumults of the world, give ear to that
voice which speaketh peace, and says, " Come unto me, all
" ye that labour and are heavy laden, and I will give you rest;
" take my yoke upon you, and ye shall find rest to your souls;
" for my yoke is easy, and my burthen is light."

VIRTUE has secret charms which all men love;
And those that do not choose her, yet approve.

TRUE happiness—man's gen'ral aim and end,
The point of rest to which our wishes tend,
To no externals ever was assign'd,
But fixt the portion of a steady mind;
A steady mind, that no desires inflame,
Still constant to itself, and still the same;
The same when fortune blows an adverse gale;
The same when on a throne or in a jail:
A mind that can each mad excess controul,
Subdue the passions, and direct the soul;
That, summon'd, chearfully resigns her breath,
Nor trembles, anxious at th' approach of death.

Epitaph upon Epictetus, the Stoic Philosopher.

" EPICTETUS, who lies here, was a slave and a crip-
" ple; poor as the beggar in the proverb, and the favourite of
" Heaven."

In

In this diftich is comprized the nobleft panegyric, and the moft important inftruction. We may learn from it, that virtue is impracticable in no condition, fince Epictetus could recommend himfelf to the regard of Heaven, amidft the temptations of poverty and flavery. Slavery has been found fo deftructive to virtue, that, in fome languages, a flave and a thief are exprefled by the fame word. And we may be admonifhed by it, not to lay any ftrefs on a man's outward circumftances, in making an eftimate of his real virtue, fince Epictetus the beggar, the cripple, and the flave, was the favourite of Heaven.

Occafioned by a Recovery from a tedious Illnefs.

FATHER Divine, Eternal One!
    While Heav'n pure homage pays,
From this dark point, beneath the fun,
    Accept a mortal's praife.
Yet what's the praife my breath can give;
    What's all that I can fay,
But that the God in whom I live
    Has giv'n me health to-day?
The theme my voice in vain affays,
    Then let my life purfue;
Let what I am record thy praife,
    Exprefs'd in what I do.
Thee more than all—and as myfelf,
    Oh teach me man to love:
Be this my fame, my glory, wealth,
    My blifs below—above!
Nor let my love to man be vain,
    My love to God be blind;
Of thee fome knowledge let me gain,
    Some blefling give mankind.
Thro' ev'ry change my life may know,
    My ebbing, flowing tides,
Firm be my faith, that all below,
    Love, join'd with wifdom, guides,
That e'en thy juftice tends to blefs,

                              Tho.

Tho' little underſtood ;
That partial evils love expreſs,
　And work the gen'ral good.
But frail, alas! this mortal clay,
　This reaſoning mind how frail!
Let ſtrength be equal to my day,
　Nor height nor depth prevail.
When o'er my roof affliction low'rs,
　Suſtain my ſinking heart ;
In all my gay, unguarded hours,
　Oh keep my better part!
And when this tott'ring fabric falls,
　Aſſiſt my ſoul to ſoar,
Where full poſſeſſion never palls,
　To know and love thee more.

THE uſe of learning is not to procure popular applauſe, or excite vain admiration, but to make the poſſeſſor more virtuous and uſeful to ſociety, and his virtue a more conſpicuous example to thoſe that are illiterate.

WHAT exalted mortal, in the laſt hour of life, would not reſign all the advantages of greatneſs and power, for a few moments of leiſure and obſcurity.

IF there is any happineſs below the ſtars, it conſiſts in a freedom from the hurry and cenſure of the world, where the mind may devote all its bright and ſerene intervals to Heaven.

THE courſe of human things is all decreed,
With each minuteſt circumſtance, above :
No fickle chance ; no blind contingencies ;
No unforeſeen events ariſe, to croſs
The purpoſes divine.————————

Hope

Hope travels through.—POPE.

THE sweet deceiver, hope, destroys,
By airy visions, real joys;
Each future scene, by her array'd
In brightness, makes the present fade,
All the long day we wish for night,
Then sigh for the return of light;
Thro' gloomy winter's reign we mourn,
'Till pleasure-pinion'd spring's return;
But here, with joyless feet, we tread
The verdant lawn, or painted mead,
'Till summer comes—yet e'en from this
Enjoyment's fled—the promis'd bliss
Is now postpon'd, 'till autumn shews
Her golden fields and loaded boughs;
Hither we press—but vain the chace!
The phantom flies with equal pace.
Now winter charms—again it comes,
And her still tasteless reign resumes;
The trav'ler thus thick mists enclose,
But seem to fly where e'er he goes.

HE is no fool, who parts with that which he cannot keep, when he is sure to be recompenced with that which he cannot lose.

THE pursuit of glory and happiness in another life, by every means of improving and exalting our own minds, becomes more and more interesting to us, the nearer we draw to the end of all sublunary enjoyments.

AS that God, whom we all adore, is a God of peace and concord, there ought to be a sacred harmony between all that profess and believe in the same Saviour.

THEY must certainly be persons of narrow and mean conceptions, who (tho' under the mask of superficial greatness of spirit) cannot raise their little ideas above pleasures familiar to their senses.   BUT

BUT the main ſtreſs of all our cares muſt lie;
To watch ourſelves with ſtrict and conſtant eye:
To mark the working mind when paſſion's courſe
Begins to ſwell, and reaſon ſtill has force ;
Or if ſhe's conquer'd by the ſtronger tide,
Obſerve the moments when they firſt ſubſide ;
For he who hopes a victory to win.
O'er other men, muſt with himſelf begin,
Elſe like a town, by mutiny oppreſs'd,
He's ruin'd by the foe within his breaſt.

ARISE my ſoul, ſurvey the morn,
And purple beauties of the dawn,
  In order as they ſhine;
The herbs that with the dew-drops glow,
The graſs, the ſhrubs, the flow'rets ſhew
  Their Maker all divine !
Hark how the warbling feather'd throng
Now tune their ſoft melodious ſong,
  From ev'ry leafy ſpray ;
The black-bird here with mellow throat
And there the thruſh with ſofter note,
  In concert pour the lay.
Do thou my ſoul reſponſive join,
Ambitious of a theme divine,
  And ſing thy Maker's praiſe :
Unnumber'd objects he ſupplies,
For contemplation's wandering eyes,
  And all the Muſes lays.

FRIENDSHIP's a pure, a Heav'n deſcended flame,
Worthy the happy region whence it came ;
The ſacred tye, that virtuous ſpirits binds,
The golden chain that links immortal minds.

--- ◇ ⬦⬦⬦⬦⬦ ◇ ---

WE ſhould never be over eager for any thing, either in our
purſuits or our prayers, leſt what we endeavour, or aſk too
violently for our intereſt, ſhould be granted us by Providence
only in order to our ruin.   Concluding

Concluding Stanzas of an Elegy on the Death of a Sister.

BUT lo! to give the unhappy mourners ease,
    From pale affliction's eye to wipe the tear;
To bid the plaintive voice of sorrow cease,
    Behold religion's Heavenly form appear.
" Attend (she cries) poor mortal! grieve no more,
    " No more lament thy dear departed friends;
" Their souls are wafted to a happier shore,
    " Where every sorrow, every trouble ends.
" Follow my steps, and soon you'll meet again,
    " Will meet in yonder blissful realms above;
" Forever there to join the seraph's strain,
    " And sing the wonders of redeeming love."

⁓⁓⁓⁓⁓⁓⁓⁓

None but the Almighty author of our beings, who knows our inmost thoughts and desires, and from whom no secrets are hid, can see into futurity: And he only knows what is best and most proper for us; if we cheerfully rely on his all-wise Providence, and confidently trust in his powerful protection, we may rest ourselves assured, that he, who is our truest friend, will guard and secure us from the many evils and dangers, which every where surround us. He will guide and direct the future events of our lives in such a manner, as will prove, by happy experience, to be the most conducive to our own good, and the most consistent with the scheme of our own happiness, both here and hereafter.

⁓⁓⁓⁓⁓⁓⁓⁓

AS some fair vi'let, loveliest of the glade,
Sheds its mild fragrance on the lonely shade,
Withdraws its modest head from public sight,
Nor courts the sun, nor seeks the glare of light;
Should some rude hand prophanely dare intrude,
And bear its beauties from its native wood,
Expos'd abroad its languid colours fly,
Its form decays, and all its odours die.

So

So woman born to dignify retreat,
Unknown to flourish, and unseen, be great ;
To give domestic life its sweetest charm,
With softness polish, and with virtue warm ;
Fearful of fame, unwilling to be known,
Should seek but Heaven's applauses and her own ;
No censures dread but those which crimes impart,
The censures of a self-condemning heart.
With angel kindness should behold distress,
And meekly pity, where she can't redress.
Like beaming mercy wipe affliction's tear,
But to herself, not justice so severe.
Her passions all corrected or subdu'd
But one—the virtuous thirst of doing good.
This great ambition still she calls her own,
This best ambition makes her breast its throne.

HAIL Power Eternal, infinite, immense,
Creator and Redeemer, Lord of life,
All good, all wise, all perfect, all divine !
Increase my ardour, elevate my soul,
And draw me from this idle, useless world,
To better thoughts—the thoughts of that to come !
Let me not beg of blessings from thy hand,
But for increase of virtue : Gracious pour
Thy Holy Spirit on my soul ; so make
Thy servant perfect, fit for Heav'n and thee :
And thou art good ! Oh guide me with thy hand,
Cure all the fond, vain evils of my heart,
And stifle every growing folly there !
Oh ! my Redeemer, kindly condescend
To hear my prayer and grant—yet wherefore speak !
If it seems good, bestow the boon I wish ;
(Thou knowest my thoughts) if not, thy will be done!

AN humble man leans not to his own understanding, he is
nsible of the deficiency of his own power and wisdom, and
usts not in it; he is also sensible of the all-sufficient power,
isdom and goodness of Almighty God, and commits him-
lf to him for counsel, guidance, direction and strength.

C   VIRTUE

VIRTUE is the higheſt exerciſe and improvement of reaſon, the integrity, the harmony and juſt balance of affection, the health, ſtrength and beauty of the mind.

WITH the talents of an angel a man may be a fool, if he judges amiſs in the ſupreme point ; judging aright in all elſe but aggravates his folly, as it ſhews him wrong, though bleſt with tne beſt capacity of being right.

WHAT a great deal of time and eaſe that man gains, who is not troubled with the ſpirit of curioſity, who lets his neighbours thoughts and behaviour alone, confines his inſpections to himſelf, and takes care of the point of honeſty and conſcience.

A MAN of true piety, that has no deſigns to carry on, like one of an eſtabliſhed fortune, always makes the leaſt noiſe. One never pulls out his money, the other never talks of religion, but when there is occaſion for it.

ADVERSITY does not make merit loſe its name, it ſerves only as a foil to virtue.

<hr>

RETIREMENT.

HOW happy he who crowns, in ſhades like theſe,
A youth of labour, with an age of eaſe ;
Who quits a world where ſtrong temptations try,
And ſince 'tis hard to combat, learns to fly !
For him no wretches born, to work and weep,
Explore the mine or tempt the dang'rous deep ;
No ſurly porter ſtands, in guilty ſtate,
To ſpurn imploring famine from the gate ;
But on he moves to meet his latter end,
Angels around befriending virtue's friend ;
Bends to the grave with unperceiv'd decay,
While reſignation gently ſlopes the way,
And all his proſpects, bright'ning to the laſt,
His Heav'n commences e'er the world be paſt !

HYMN

HYMN to the EVENING.

E'ER the fun's declining ray
    Has left yon' diftant fky,
And the parting ftreak of day
    Has fhut upon the eye—
Come, modeft ev'ning, kindly fpread
    Thy dufk-enfabled veft,
And teach reflective thought to fpread
    Devotion on the breaft.
Oh ! lift the mind to blefs the pow'r,
    Whofe mem'ry ftill fhall laft,
And bid him ferve the prefent hour,
    Whofe madnefs loft the paft.
Inftructive, tell the pomp of ftate,
    The pride of mighty blood,
That none are ever truly great,
    That are not truly good.
To all one admonition give,
    Unfearful of reply,
That he alone deferves to live,
    Who beft prepares to die.

    WHEN modeft merit feems to fhun that praife
Th' admiring world to merit ever pays,
It takes, unknowingly, the road to fame,
And, by declining, gains a furer name.

    BE mine to live in private blifs,
Safe and obfcure in fome recefs,
Since faction and high-minded ftrife
But fhake the peaceful lake of life ;
And better is the little home,
Where confcious fafety cheers the dome.

A PRAYER of PRINCE EUGENE.

  I BELIEVE in thee, oh my God ! do thou ftrengthen
my faith ; I hope in thee, confirm my hope ; I love thee, in-
                                   flame

flame my love more and more; I repent of all my sins, but do thou increase my repentance. As my first beginning, I worship thee; as my last end, I long for thee; as my eternal benefactor, I praise thee; and as my supreme protector, I pray unto thee, that it may please thee, O Lord! to guide and lead me by thy providence; to keep me in obedience to thy justice; to comfort me by thy mercy; and to protect me by thy almighty power. I submit unto thee all my thoughts, words and deeds, as well as my afflictions, pains and sufferings; and I desire to have thee always in my mind, to do all my works in thy name, and for thy sake to bear all adversity with patience. I will nothing, but what thou willest, O God! because it is agreeable unto thee. O give me grace, that I may be attentive in my prayer, temperate in my diet, vigilant in my conduct, and immoveable in all good purposes. Grant, most merciful Lord! that I may be true and faithful to those who have entrusted me with their secrets; that I may be courteous and kind towards all men; and that both in my words and actions I may shew unto them a good example. Dispose my heart to praise and admire thy goodness; to hate all errors and evil works; to love my neighbour; and to despise the world. Assist me, good God! in subduing lust by mortification; covetousness by liberality; anger by mildness; and lukewarmness by zeal and fervency. Enable me to conduct myself with prudence in all transactions; and to shew courage in danger; patience in adversity; and in prosperity an humble mind. Let thy grace illuminate my understanding; direct my will; sanctify my body; and bless my soul. Make me diligent in curbing all irregular affections; zealous in imploring thy grace; careful in keeping thy commandments; and constant in working out my own salvation. Finally, O God! make me sensible, how little is the world; how great thy Heavens; how short time; and how long will be the blessed eternity. O! that I may well prepare myself for death; that I may dread thy judgments; that I may avoid the torments of hell; and obtain of thee, O God! eternal life, thro' the merits of Jesus Christ our Lord. Amen.

THERE is one sure way of pleasing in company, which is in every one's power to practise, viz. shewing a disposition to be pleased.
IT

I T often happens, that thofe are moft defirous of governing others, who are leaft able to govern themfelves.

I T is indeed a ferious thing to die ; but virtue difarms the gloomy king of all his terrors, and brightens the profpect of futurity.

SENECA fays, there is no difference betwixt poffeffing a thing and not defiring it.

VAIN are all forms prefcrib'd by art,
    All outward modes of worfhip vain ;
An honeft, gen'rous, pious heart,
    Can only true acceptance gain.

FAREWELL, ye vain, I hate your ways,
    Ye grov'ling fons of pride, adieu ;
Poor av'rice, how thy hope decays !
    Thy fteps I tremble to purfue.
To Sion's hill I lift my eye,
    To Sion's hill direct my feet ;
From all things learn to live and die,
    From all the vile and vain retreat.

The character of the Lady of one of the antient Earls of Weft-moreland, written by her hufband, and infcribed in the chimney-wall of a large room, at Budftone Place, in Kent, once the feat of that noble family.

S H E feared God, and knew how to ferve him; fhe affigned times for her devotion, and kept them ; fhe was a perfect wife, and a true friend ; fhe joyed moft to oblige thofe neareft and deareft to me ; fhe was ftill the fame, ever kind and never troublefome ; often preventing my defires ; difputing none ; providently managing all that was mine ; living in appearance above mine eftate, while fhe advanced it ; fhe was of a great

fpirit ;

spirit ; facetly tempered ; of a sharp wit ; without offence ; of excellent speech ; blest with silence ; of a chearful temper ; mildly governed ; of a brave fashion to win respect, and to daunt boldness ; pleasing to all of her sex ; intimate with few ; delighting in the best ; ever avoiding all persons and places in their honour blemished ; and was as free from doing ill as giving the occasion. She died as she lived, well ; and blest in the greatest extremity ; most patiently sending forth her pure soul with many zealous prayers and hymns to her Maker ; pouring out her affectionate heart in passionate streams to her Saviour.—**********************

N. B. The beginning and ending of this inscription being defaced by time, the date is uncertain.

MAN may, in scenes of ev'ry kind,
Fit lessons of instruction find :
The bird, for injury and wrong,
Repays th' oppressor with a song ;
Oh ! blush to think, that, Heav'n inspir'd,
Thy breast should be with malice fir'd !
Learn hence thy passion to restrain,
And still that god-like rule maintain,
To seek no vengeance on a foe,
But bless the hand that gives the blow.

IF you desire to live in peace and honour, in favour with God and man, and to die in the glorious hope of rising from the grave to a life of endless happiness—if these things appear worthy your ambition, you must set out in earnest in the pursuit of them. Virtue and happiness are not attainable by chance, nor by a cold and languid approbation ; they must be sought with ardour, attended to with diligence, and every assistance must be eagerly embraced that may enable you to obtain them.

TO

T O take sincere pleasure in the blessings and excellencies of others, is a much surer mark of benevolence than to pity their calamities.

EQUALLY vain and absurd Is every scheme of life that is not subservient to, and does not terminate in that great end of our being, the attainment of real excellence, and of the favour of God. Whenever this becomes sincerely our object, then will pride and vanity, envy, ambition, covetousness, and every evil passion, lose their power over us ; and we shall, in the language of scripture, " walk humbly with our God."

Extract from a Poem called antient and modern Rome.

REFLECTION hath its joy, a pensive calm
That shrouds the soul, and bears it on the wings
Of vagrant thought, to mem'ry's wide domain !
Now let's indulge it, while we here remark
The mad career of fortune, and behold
Imperial Rome, 'midst all her triumphs, fall'n !
So closes ev'ry scene, and thus decay
The works of man—allow'd a little space
To shine, attract, then fade, and be forgot !
For see the paths that lead to pow'r, and fame,
And those which feel the peasant's silent step,
End in one point ; observe ambition's flight,
And laugh at all the wild fantastic dreams
Of human folly. Seeking then thy arms,
Oh, virtue ! let us court thee as our good ;
Our only treasure, and our only hope ;
Our shield, to guard us 'gainst a faithless world,
And all its poison'd arrows : Thou unhurt,
Sprung from immortal truth, serenely bright,
Sustain'st the general wreck ; and like the sun
Shalt still appear with undiminish'd light,
When all the boasted monuments of pride
Shall sink, and mingle with the dust they hid !

HABITUAL

HABITUAL evils are not quickly chang'd ;
But many days muſt paſs, and many ſorrows,
Conſcious remorſe, and anguiſh muſt be felt,
To curb deſire, to break the ſtubborn will,
And work a ſecond nature in the ſoul,
'Ere virtue can reſume the place ſhe loſt :
'Tis elſe diſſimulation.————— —————

IN the works of man, perfection is aimed at, but it can only
be found in thoſe of the Creator.

CONSCIENCE is the law of the all-wiſe author of nature, written on our hearts, or properly the application of this
law, as it regards the judgments we ſhould form of particular
actions.—It is like a cenſor noting and obſerving our actions,
and therefore it has not undeſervedly been called by ſome a portion of the virgin ſoul, as not admitting the leaſt blemiſh of
prevarication. Hence good actions beget ſecurity in the conſcience, but bad cauſe anguiſh and vexation, which is better
known by experience than explained by words : For, if it is
painful to us to abide by the judgments of thoſe we live with,
and to put up with their reprehenſions, it will be more ſo to
be condemned by our own reaſon, and to carry about us ſo ſe-
vere a judge of our actions. And thus it is, that conſcience
performs the function both of a witneſs and judge, when it re-
primands us for having done amiſs, as Juvenal ſays——

Not ſharp revenge, nor hell itſelf can find
A fiercer torment than a guilty mind ;
Which day and night does dreadfully accuſe,
Condemns the wretch, and ſtill the charge renews.

RICHES, alas ! are tranſient things,
  And titles but an airy dream ;
Our pleaſures flow from nobler ſprings,
  And give more laſting peace than them.
Let ſordid mortals hope for wealth,
  This never ſhall my pray'r employ ;
Give me but competence and health,
  I envy not their ſhort-liv'd joy.

PRIDE

PRIDE AND HUMILITY.

MARK how the stately tree difdainful rears
His tow'ring head, and mingles with the clouds!
But by his fatal height the more expos'd
To all the fury of the raging ftorm ;
His honours fly, the fport of angry winds,
'Till the loud blaft, with direful ftroke, defcends :
Torn from his bafis, low on earth he lies,
And the hills echo to the founding fall.
So pride with haughty port, defies in vain
The force of rough adverfity, which rends,
With double violence, the ftubborn heart.
   But like a tender plant humility
Bends low before the threat'ning blaft, unhurt
Eludes its rage, and lives through all the ftorm.
   Pride is the liv'ry of the prince of darknefs,
Worn by his flaves, who glory in their fhame ;
A gaudy drefs, but tarnifh'd, rent, and foul,
And loathfome to the holy eye of Heav'n.
   But fweet humility, a fhining robe,
Beftow'd by Heav'n upon its fav'rite fons ;
The robe which God approves, and angels wear ;
Fair 'femblance of the glorious prince of light,
Who ftoop'd to dwell (divine humility !)
With finful worms, and poverty, and fcorn.
Pride is the fource of difcord, ftrife and war,
And all the endlefs train of heavy woes
Which wait on wretched man ! the direful fting
Of envy, and the dreaded frowns of fcorn,
And gloomy difcontent, and black defpair.
   But fweet humility, the fource of peace,
Of amity and love, content and joy ;
Where fhe refides a thoufand bleffings wait
To gild our lives, and form a Heav'n below.
   Pride leads her wretched vot'ries to contempt,
To certain ruin, infamy and death.
   But fweet humility points out the way
To happinefs, and life, and lafting honours.

Humility, how glorious ! how divine !
Thus cloath'd and thus enrich'd, O may I fhine ;
Be mine this treafure, this celeftial robe,
And let the fons of pride poffefs the globe.

WHAT walls can bound, or what compelling rein,
Th' ungovern'd luft of avarice reftrain ?
Wealth he has none, who mourns his fcanty ftore,
And 'midft of plenty ftarves, and thinks he's poor.

WHEN Ulyffes entrufted the education of his fon to the nobles of Ithaca, " O my friends," faid he, " if ever you " loved his father, fhew it in your care towards him ; but " above all, do not omit to form him juft, fincere, and faith- " ful in keeping a fecret."

THE fureft way to purchafe happinefs, muft be, to let as little of our time as poffible flip away unobferved and unimproved.

VARIOUS are the innocent diverfions of life, by which we may lengthen time in general, and prevent any part of it to be ufelefs, or tedious.

BEFORE you make an abfolute promife, weigh all the confequences of keeping it ; but, when once you have made it, let the circumftances be important, or ever fo trifling, hold it as facred ; and never be influenced to break it, unlefs the making it good prove injurious to virtue.

THE table of a good œconomift, is always attended with neatnefs, plenty and chearfulnefs. When we have provided enough to maintain us, in the order fuitable to our character, we ought to be proportionably hofpitable ; but the more we live within decent bounds, the more of our fortune may be converted to noble ufes.

HE

H E that keeps not open a conftant intercourfe with Heaven, by frequent fervors of rational devotion, knows not the fublimeft joy.

T H E R E are attractions in modeft diffidence, above the force of words. A filent addrefs is the genuine eloquence of fincerity.

·····◇·····◇···◁◇◁◇◁◇◁◇◁◇···◇·····◇···

W H O look on difappointments, toils and ftrife,
And all the confequential ills of life,
Not as feverities, or caufelefs woes,
But eafy terms indulgent Heav'n allows
To man, by fhort probation to obtain
Immortal recompence for tranfient pain;
The intent of Heav'n, thus rightly underftood,
From ev'ry evil we extract a good;
This truth divine, implanted in the heart,
Supports each drudging mortal thro' his part;
Gives a delightful profpect to the blind,
The friendlefs thence a conftant fuccour find;
The wretch, by fraud betray'd, by power opprefs'd,
With this reftorative, ftill fooths his breaft;
This fuffering virtue chears, this pain beguiles,
And decks calamity herfelf in fmiles.

·····◇·····◇···◁◇◁◇◁◇◁◇◁◇···◇·····◇···

W H E R E V E R a great deal of gratitude is found in a poor man, it may be taken for granted there would be as much generofity, if he were a rich man.

A D D I S O N, after a long and manly, but vain ftruggle with his diftemper, difmiffed his phyficians, and with them all hopes of life; but with his hopes of life, he difmiffed not his concern for the living, but fent for a youth nearly related and finely accomplifhed, but not above being the better for good impreffions from a dying friend; he came, and life now glimmering in the focket, the dying friend was filent; after a de-

cent and proper paufe, the youth faid, " dear fir! you fent
" for me I believe, and I hope that you have fome commands;
" if you have, I fhall hold them moft facred." May diftant
ages not only hear but feel the reply!—Forcibly grafping
the youth's hand, he foftly faid, " fee in what peace a Chrif-
" tian can die." He fpoke with difficulty, and foon expired.
Thro' grace divine, how great is man! thro' divine mercy how ftinglefs death! who would not thus expire?

BLEST folitude! how fweet thy peaceful fcenes!
　Where contemplation's vot'ries love to ftray;
Where in her fapient drefs, religion reigns,
　And fhines more fplendid than the noontide ray.

LET angry zealots quarrel for a name,
The good, the juft, the virtuous are the fame;
Virtue and grace are not to fects confin'd,
They blend with all, and fpread amongft mankind.
And the pure flame that warms the pious breaft,
Thofe cannot merit who condemn the reft.

THE terms of charity are never hard,
Love and compaffion are their own reward;
A foul that fuccours virtue when diftreft,
Can with reflection make a noble feaft,
Which nourifhes the mind, and overpays
A gen'rous deed with felf-approving praife.

WHAT can the man fear, who takes care in all his actions to pleafe a Being that is omnipotent?—A Being who is
able to crufh all his adverfaries?—A Being that can divert any
misfortune from befalling him, or turn any fuch misfortune
to his advantage? The perfon who lives with this conftant
and habitual regard to the great fuperintendant of the world,
is indeed fure that no real evil can come into his lot. Bleffings may appear under the fhape of pains, loffes and difappointments; but let him have patience, and he will fee them

in

in their proper figures. Dangers may threaten him, but he may reft fatisfied, that they will either 'not reach him, or that if they do, they will be the inftruments of good to him. In fhort, he may look upon all croffes and accidents, fufferings and afflictions, as meam which are made ufe of to bring him to happinefs.

ALL the ways of growing rich, are equal to perfons greedy of gain. Riches, in their efteem, obtain the place of equity, reputation, their friends, relations, and frequently their God.

THE WISH.

I ASK not fortune's partial fmile,
    Exhauftlefs fource of care;
Not all her fancied gay delights
    Can claim a ferious prayer.
Nor pleafure's foft alluring form,
    With ardent wifh I feek;
Far lefs the captivating bloom
    That glows on beauty's cheek.
I afk not, that in calm repofe
    My even days may flow,
Unruffled by adverfity,
    Exempt from human woe.
Enough that no reflections keen,
    No crimes my foul opprefs,
To rob me of the flattering hope
    Of future happinefs.
But grant me that bleft frame of mind,
    Where no vain thoughts intrude;
That bleft ferenity which fprings
    From confcious rectitude.

THE love of pleafure has fo blinded the eyes of the prefent age, that they cannot fee clearly the fatisfaction of a pure and rational life.   D   WHEN

WHEN you fee the choler of a friend begin to kindle, if you would do good, throw water thereon to cool, not wood to inflame it.

NO fimple cuftom is more blamable, than that of lying fhut up in the arms of floth and darknefs, when the cheerful return of day invites the whole creation to joy and bufinefs. Sleep, any further than as it is a neceffary refrefhment, is the poorest, dullest state of exiftence we can be in ; and it is fo far from being a real enjoyment, that it bears the neareft refemblance of death, and carries all the horrors of oblivion in it. We are forced to receive it, either in a ftate of infenfibility, or in the delufive folly of dreams. Sleep, when too much humoured, gives a foftnefs and idlenefs to all our tempers ; and no fluggifh perfon can be qualified, or difpofed, to enter into the true fpirit of prayer, or the exercife of any active virtue.

IT is not when misfortunes come upon us, the time to fet about the philofophy of bearing, or the refignation of fubmitting to them ; it is in health we fhould prepare ourfelves againft ficknefs.

IF affectation could be entirely banifhed, how few, in comparifon with the prefent ftate of things, would be the number of prepofterous miftakes.

THE niceft rule in œconomy, is to make our being one uniform and confiftent fcene of innocent pleafures, and moderate cares ; and not to be tranfported with joy on occafions of good fortune, or too much dejected, in circumftances of diftrefs.

VAGRANT defires, and impertinent mirth, will be too apt to engage our minds unlefs we can poffefs ourfelves in that fobriety of heart, which is above all tranfient pleafures, and which will fix our affections on things above.

━━◇━━◇━━◇◎◎◎◎◎◎◎◎◇━━◇━━◇━━

—————————BEHOLD, fond man !
See here thy pictur'd life : Pafs fome few years ;
Thy flow'ring fpring, thy fummer's ardent ftrength,　Thy

Thy fober autumn fading into age,
And pale-concluding winter comes at laft
And fhuts the fcene.—Ah! whither now are fled,
Thofe dreams of greatnefs? thofe unfolid hopes
Of happinefs? thofe longings after fame?
Thofe reftlefs cares? thofe bufy buftl'ing days?
Thofe gay-fpent feftive nights? thofe varying thoughts
Loft between good and ill, that fhar'd thy life?
All now are fled! Religion fole remains
Immortal, never-failing friend of man,
His guide to happinefs on high.

I F people took as much pains to be good, as they do to appear fo, they would, through grace, bring about their purpofe.

G O D the Lord and Father of all, has given no one of his children fuch a property in his peculiar portion of the things of this world, but that he has given his needy brother a right in the furplufage of his goods; fo that it cannot juftly be denied him, when his preffing wants call for it.

W H O is wife? He that learns from every one. Who is powerful? He that governs his paffions. Who is rich? He that is content.

FIX'D in the fhade of this imperfect ftate,
'Tis ours, fubmiffive, better fcenes to wait,
And plaintive mufing on each various pain,
Or o'er the pebbly brook or on the plain;
In love with nature, let us, while we ftay,
To nature's parent true devotion pay;
By him foon fummon'd, fhall we take our flight,
Far to the realms of uncreated light.

TRANSPORTING period! when wilt thou appear?
Thou blifsful dawn of that immortal day,

That

That ne'er shall see a dusky ev'ning spread
To veil its light; which ne'er shall need the sun,
Nor stars, nor glimm'ring moon, to cheer its shade.
    Ye fair inhabitants of blissful seats,
Unfold your golden gates, and call me hence;
Sick of this mortal state, this round of error,
Of darkness and mistake, I long for rest.

    T H Y force alone, religion, death disarms,
Breaks all his darts, and every viper charms.
Soften'd by thee, the grisly form appears
No more the horrid object of our fears.
We, undismay'd, this awful pow'r obey,
That guides us thro' the safe, tho' gloomy way,
Which leads to life.————————————

    T H E advantages of frequent thoughts of death are certain-
ly unspeakable; and most erroneous is the notion, that gloomi-
ness must be the consequence of such meditation.

    I T most certainly becomes us, as we are rational and mor-
tal, to consider the high things expected of us as rationals; and
the haste we ought to make in accomplishing them as we are
mortal; and it would bespeak us wise, as we ourselves would
receive the benefit, if we, with great seriousness and attention,
pondered over and meditated upon that, which must, 'ere long,
be our lot; that hour, which high and low, rich and poor,
must all arrive at; and by which the beggar and the prince
will be levelled with the dust.

    L E T prudence always attend your pleasures; it is the way
to enjoy the sweets of them, and not to be afraid of the conse-
quences.

    C O M P A N Y and cheerfulness are necessary, and of use;
but a constant course of mirth betrays such a levity of mind,
that your presence will never be desired, but to divert others,
whose regard ceases the instant the laughter is over; and should
your wit offend, you may be assured of an enemy.

I F

IF you have any good quality, do not make eulogiums your-self upon it, as it will not be credited upon your word only.

WE have to do with one whose power is unbounded, whose knowledge is infinite, and whose justice is perfect ; therefore from him we can hide no guilt ; we can fly to no place of de-fence, nor can we expect acceptance, but in the paths of reason and religion ; in them we shall find the highest pleasure, and join to the cheerful enjoyment of the things of this world, the pros-pect of a continuance and encrease of pleasures when this world has no more to give.

SHORT is the date and narrow is the span,
Which bounds the little life of foolish man.
Gay scenes of bliss the ravish'd soul surprize,
Raise his vain hopes, and glitter in his eyes ;
Of swelling titles he supinely dreams,
Vast are his projects, and refin'd his schemes ;
But when his morning views of joy are past,
The melancholy ev'ning comes at last ;
The tyrant, death, a hasty summons sends,
And all his momentary glory ends.

SINCE then old time steals all away,
Take heed the sunshine of your day
    Nought but true joys may find :
To proper use apply what's sent ;
For know no beauty's permanent,
    But beauty of the mind.

THE life of man is compared to the herbage of the field, but a shadow is a more striking emblem ; and the flux of time, measured by a shadow, is a lesson that teaches us the necessity of preparing ourselves for a more permanent state.

AS too long a retirement weakens the mind, so too much company dissipates it. It is good sometimes to recollect one's
self;

felf; nay, it is even neceffary to give an exact account of one's words and thoughts to one's felf; and of the progrefs we have made in wifdom. A man that would reap the fruits of reading and converfation, and improve by what he has feen, muft be no ftranger to filence, repofe and meditation.

AS arrogance and conceitednefs of our own abilities are very difguftful to men of fenfe and virtue, we may be fure they are highly difpleafing to that being who delights in an humble mind.

THE reproofs of a relation may be thought to proceed from an affectation of fuperiority; of an enemy, from a fpirit of malice; and of an indifferent perfon, from pride or impertinence, and fo be flighted: But when they come from one who loves us, and come armed with all the tender concern that an unfeigned affection is known to dictate, they ought of courfe to take effect, and become irrefiftible.

IT is poffible to be happy in the abfence of all that people call amufement and diverfion. When the mind is in a fituation fuperior to the changing fcenes below the fun, in purfuit of boundlefs and immortal blifs, the foul, with a noble freedom, afcends the celeftial heights, in fearch of its great original, the fountain of its exiftence, and centre of all its hopes.

ON CONTENTMENT.

O THOU! whofe pow'r can fharpeft grief affuage,
Or ftop the torrent of impetuous rage;
Contentment, hear; Oh liften to my ftrain!
Nor let the mufe implore thy aid in vain;
Teach me thro' life's advent'rous paths to go,
T' enjoy the good, and calmly bear the woe;
To view unmov'd the mifer's hoarded ftore,
Without a figh, or greedy wifh for more;
To fcorn the pomp, and pageantry of ftate,
The empty fhew, and titles of the great,

Grant

Grant me to live a peaceful, rural life,
Remote from envy and tumultuous strife ;
There may I pass each hour by ⬤tue's rules,
Nor vainly seek th' applauding breath of fools.

G L I D E on securely, wisely tread,
The paths where truth and virtue lead.
It matters not how great the man,
If all's confin'd to life's short span ;
It matters not how rich or poor,
Peace is no gift in human pow'r ;
They find her who contented dwell
In the cool grot or mossy cell.

━◆━◈━◈━◈━◈━◈━◆━

T O keep the passions of others submissive, there is a necessity of triumphing over one's own ; to oblige them to be virtuous, one must set the example and be the model : There is
not a better lesson than that, which a superior makes it his duty
to practise.

T H E R E is so great a grace and authority in virtue, that
it never fails to attract the esteem even of those that are most
abandoned to vice and immorality ; so that religion, by its
own authority, and the reasonable force of it, is sufficent to
establish its empire in the mind of any thinking person.

L E T your expectations be higher than any dignity or enjoyment this world can boast. Let a celestial crown fire your
ambition ; and in the pursuit of infinite happiness, grasp at nothing below the glories of immortality. With what a divine
ambition does the prospect of Heavenly joys inspire the soul.
If you are reckoned by any of the gay and giddy world the less
polite for entertaining such exalted thoughts of pleasure, be
content in being unfashionably good, since thereby you can
keep your peace ; be fearless and open to the inspection of
Heaven ; justify yourself to your own conscience, and secure
the divine interest. Be always assured, that no character is
more amiable, than that of a female, who in the gayest bloom

of

of youth, and triumph of beauty, practises the rules of purity and virtue ; and that in the exercise of those qualities the finest breeding confists.

IN all things preserve integrity ; the confcioufnefs of thy own uprightnefs will alleviate the toil of bufinefs, and foften the harfhnefs of ill fuccefs and difappointments, and give thee an humble confidence before God, when the ingratitude of man, or the iniquity of the times, may rob thee of other due reward.

THE time of ficknefs or affliction is like the cool of the day was to Adam, a feafon of peculiar propriety for the voice of God to be heard ; and may be improved into a very advantageous opportunity of begetting or encreafing fpiritual life in the foul.

LIFE is SHORT.

Man's life, like any weavers' fhuttle flies,
Or like a tender flowret fades and dies ;
Or like a race it ends without delay,
Or like a vapour vanifhes away ;
Or like a candle which each moment waftes,
Or like a veffel under fail it haftes ;
Or like a poft it gallops very faft,
Or like the fhadow of a cloud 'tis paft.
Our caftle is but weak, and ftrong the foe,
Our breath is fhort, our death is certain too ;
But as his coming is a fecret ftill,
Let us be ready, come death when he will.

Concluding Stanzas of a Piece wrote on Recovery from Sicknefs.

FATHER of life ! whofe arm with equal power,
    And equal goodnefs, can deprefs or raife ;
Complete the bleffings thou haft deign'd to fhow'r,
    And grant encreafing worth to length of days.

Oh !

Oh! grant me still to trust thy tender care,
  In humble praise to use this added breath,
In health, the innocence of sickness wear,
  And keep, thro' life, the sober thoughts of death.

A WISE Heathen, with great justice, compares prosperity to the indulgence of a fond mother to her child, which often proves his ruin; but the affection of the Divine Being to that of a wise father, who would have his sons exercised with labour, disappointment and pains, that they may gather strength and improve their fortitude. Sometimes too, a misfortune may happen to a good man, to preserve him from a much greater one. Thus sickness may be a very great mercy to him, if it keeps him from embarking in a vessel which will be lost in its passage. Thus poverty may screen him from a great many evils which would be brought upon him by riches, and the like. We are so short-sighted, that we know not how to distinguish, and often take the greatest blessings for misfortunes, and the heaviest curses for blessings. We are like mariners, who by fair winds might run into the way of pirates; but by those contrary to their wishes, reach their port in safety.

Extempore Exclamation on the Prospect of Winter.

O H! may our follies, like the falling trees,
  Be stript of ev'ry leaf by autumn's wind;
May ev'ry branch of vice embrace the breeze,
  And nothing leave but virtue's fruit behind.
Then when old age, life's winter, shall appear,
  In conscious hope, all future ills we'll brave,
With fortitude our dissolution bear,
  And sink, forgotten, in the silent grave.

THE man within the golden mean,
Who can his boldest wish contain,
Securely views the ruin'd cell,
Where sordid want and sorrow dwell,
And in himself, serenely great,
Declines an envied room of state.

IT

I T is a melancholy confideration, that our comforts often produce our greateft anxieties ; and that an encreafe of our poffeffions is but an inlet to new difquietudes.

W E A K and feeble minds are moft prone to anger, and by their exceeding fiercenefs, generally difappoint their own purpofe ; but the greateft and braveft of men, are always calm and fedate ; they are above being difturbed with little injuries, and can generoufly pardon the greateft ; taking more delight in mercy and forgivenefs, than in profecuting revenge when it is in their power.

O T H E R vices are confined within certain bounds, and have a particular object, but affectation diffufes itfelf over the whole man, and infects the good qualities both of body and mind.

S H U N the leaft appearance of evil, that you may not be fufpected ; and if you cannot avoid both, choofe rather to be fufpected, when you do not deferve it, than to do evil, without being fufpected.

B E very cautious of fpeaking or believing any ill of your neighbours ; but be much more cautious of making hafty reports of them to their difadvantage.

L E T virtue and innocence accompany your recreations ; for unlawful pleafures, tho' agreeable for a moment, are too often attended with bad confequences ; and inftead of relaxing the mind, plunge us into an abyfs of trouble and affliction.

F I L I A L, fubmiffive to the fov'reign will,
Glad of the good—and patient of the ill,
I'll work, in narrow fphere, what Heav'n approves,
Abating hatreds, and encreafing loves ;
My friendfhips, ftudies, pleafures all my own,
Alike to envy and to fame unknown ;
Such in fome bleft afylum let me lie,
Take off my fill of life, and wait, not wifh to die.

WHEN

WHEN beauty's charms decay, as foon they muft,
And all its glories humbled in the duft,
The virtuous mind, beyond the rage of time,
Shall ever bloffom in a happier clime,
Whofe never-fading joys no tongue can tell,
Where everlafting youth and beauty dwell ;
Where pain and forrow never more fhall move,
But all is pleafure, harmony and love.

SEARCHING after HAPPINESS.

OH! happinefs, thou pleafing dream,
    Where is thy fubftance found ?
Sought through the varying fcenes in vain,
    Of earth's capacious round.
The charms of grandeur, pomp and fhew,
    Are nought but gilded fnares ;
Ambition's painful fteep afcent,
    Thick fet with thorny cares.
The bufy town, the crowded ftreet,
    Where noife and difcord reign,
We gladly leave, and tir'd, retreat,
    To breath and thinke again.
Yet, if retirement's pleafing charms
    Detain the captive mind,
The foft enchantment foon diffolves,
    'Tis empty all as wind.
Religion's facred lamp alone,
    Unerring points the way,
Where happinefs forever fhines,
    With unpolluted ray ;
To regions of eternal peace,
    Beyond the ftarry fkies,
Where pure, fublime, and perfect joys,
    In endlefs profpect rife.

OH would'ft thou, man! but now and then defcend
Into the dark receffes of thy breaft,

                Before

Before the seeds of baleful vice have sprung,
And tak'n possession of thy easy heart ;
Then might'st thou think on other worlds to come,
And live in solitude without a fear.

HAPPY the man! whose tranquil mind,
Sees nature in her changes kind,
    And pleas'd the whole surveys ;
For him the morn benignly smiles,
And evening shades reward the toils,
    That measure out his days.
The varying year may shift the scene,
The sounding tempests lash the main,
    And Heaven's own thunders roll ;
Calmly he sees the bursting storm,
Tempests nor thunder can deform
    The morning of his soul.

THE industrious ant, by nature taught,
With more than common prudence fraught,
Lays up secure an annual store,
(It's little date, perhaps no more :)
Would man (who Lord of all presides,
Alone whom reason's influence guides,
Whom Heav'n, in mercy unconfin'd,
For nobler purposes design'd)
Thus hoard against that common state
We all must prove, or soon or late;
How calm might he resign his breath,
And smiling, meet the arm of death !
With joy his soul to Heav'n commend,
And fearless, wait his latter end.

NOT all the gifts of wealth, the pomp of state,
The gilded palace, or the envied throne,
Deserve the real tribute of applause.
Praise rather those who steadily pursue
The precepts of humility, who hear
The voice of cooler reason, nor desire
More than their flocks, and herds, the tufted cell,

Or

Or mofs-grown cottage, the abode of peace :
They fteer fecurely down life's placid ftream,
Rich in themfelves, and crown'd with length of days.

— ⬦ ⬦⬦⬦⬦⬦⬦⬦ ⬦ —

TEMPORAL things more ravifh in the expectation,
than in fruition ; but things eternal, more in the fruition than
expectation.

VIRTUE is the greateft ornament ; it is to the young
neceffary, to the aged comfortable, to the poor ferviceable, to
the rich an ornament, to the fortunate an honour, to the un-
fortunate a fupport. She ennobles the flave, and exalts nobility itfelf. In fhort, let it be remembered, that none can be
difciples of the graces but in the fchool of virtue ; and that
thofe who wifh to be lovely, muft learn to be good.

— ⬦ ⬦⬦⬦⬦⬦⬦⬦ ⬦ —

THE folid joys of human kind,
Are thofe that flow from peace of mind,
For who the fweets of life can tafte,
With vice and tim'rous guilt oppreft ?
'Tis virtue foftens all our toils,
    With peace our confcience crowns ;
Gives pleafure when our fortune fmiles,
    And courage when it frowns ;
Calms ev'ry trouble, makes the foul ferene,
Smooths the contracted brow, and cheers the heart within.

— ⬦ ⬦⬦⬦⬦⬦⬦⬦ ⬦ —

OH virtue, how lovely are thy charms ! not half fo fair the
beauteous blufhes of the morn, the flowery meads, or all the
cheering verdure of the groves.

THE man who has fo little knowledge of human nature, as
to feek happinefs by changing any thing, but his own difpofitions, will wafte his life in fruitlefs efforts, and multiply the
griefs which he purpofes to remove.

E   THERE

THERE can be no true and sincere pleasure in any sinful and vicious course, tho' it be attended with all the pomp and splendour of outward happiness and prosperity ; for wherever sin or vice is, there must be guilt ; and wherever guilt is, the mind will be restless and unquiet.

⬥⬥⬥⬥⬥⬥⬥⬥⬥

PURE are the joys above the skies,
  And all the regions peace ;
No wanton lips nor envious eyes,
  Can see or taste the bliss.
These holy gates forever bar
  Pollution, sin and shame ;
None shall obtain admittance there,
  But followers of the Lamb.

O THOU, supremely wise, supremely good !
Whose ways are like th' unfathomable flood,
Grant me to celebrate thy glorious name,
'Till death dissolves this late preserved frame ;
And when this earth shall hasten to decay,
When seas shall burn, and mountains melt away ;
When suns and stars, in wild confusion hurl'd,
Now crush each other now destroy a world,
May I resume the sacred theme above,
Forever praise thee, and forever love.

HAIL, moderation ! virtue, Heav'nly bright,
Thou shining path, thou ever glorious light !
Steer'd and conducted by thy certain thread,
The lab'rinth of life we safely tread ;
And with a sure unerring eye survey,
The various perils of our painful way ;
From thee alone the mighty blessings flow,
To double pleasure and to lessen woe ;
In every case t' apply the healing balm,
And sooth out stormy passions to a calm.

OF all the calamities to which the condition of mortality exposes mankind, the loss of reason appears, to those who have the least spark of humanity, by far the most dreadful; and they behold that last stage of human wretchedness with deeper commiseration than any other.

THE forgiving of injuries, is a virtue which not only Christianity, but morality enforces. The Heathens practised it to admiration; the primitive Christians exceeded them: But what a glorious example have we in the Lord and Master of our salvation, who prayed for his crucifiers—" Father, forgive them," &c. Luke xxiii. 34.

A Wife man will defire no more, than what he may get justly, use soberly, distribute cheerfully, and leave contentedly.

EXPENSIVE drefs is not a crime, because there is any harm in good apparel; but because it shews a depravity of mind, which turns the necessary use of clothes into extravagance, pride and folly.

O 'TIS a Heav'nly virtue, when the heart
Can feel the forrows of another's bosom!
It dignifies the man. The stupid wretch,
Who knows not this sensation, is an image,
And wants the feeling to make up a life.

SHORT is, the date of our existence here,
As the light rain-bow in the lucid sphere;
Tho' sacred science all her stores expand,
Tho' wealth and honour flow from fortune's hand;
Tho' every virtue in progression rife,
To make us learn'd, benevolent and wife;
Tho' great in title, and renown'd in birth,
Our last retreat's to the oblivious earth.

THOU Pow'r Supreme! whose influence benign,
O'er all creation's infinite extent
Shines forth ineffable, inspire my heart

With

With kindnefs univerfal ; let not pride,
Envy malignant, fordid luft of gain,
Or any kindred difcord-brooding vice,
Difturb my tranquil breaft, but let me pafs
Thro' all the varied fcenes which life unfolds,
In focial harmony with all around,
Serene and calm as glides the lucid ftream.

REPUTATIONS are of a fubtile, infinuating nature—
like water, derived from the cleareft fpring, when it chances
to mix with a foul current, it runs undiftinguifhed in one
muddy ftream ; and they both partake of the fame colour and
condition. If we keep bad company, however little we may
be criminal in reality, we muft expect the fame cenfure that
is due to the worft of our affociates.

HUMILITY is a virtue, which highly adorns the
character in which it refides, and fets off every other virtue ;
it is an admirable ingredient of a contented mind, and an excellent fecurity againft many of thofe ills in life, which are
moft fenfibly felt by people of a delicate nature.

THAT man is moft bleffed, who receives his daily bread with
gratitude and thankfulnefs from the hand of God ; and he who
does, experiences a pleafure that exceeds defcription. It is this
that gives a relifh to every repaft ; it is this that makes the
coarfeft morfel delicious to the tafte ; and it is the want of this
that makes affluence a burthen, inftead of a bleffing to the rich.

THE fleep of the labouring man is fweet ; and if he toil
hard for the bread that perifheth, he has, in the midft of every
want, if a follower of Chrift, bread to eat that the world
knows nothing of. It is not faid, happy are they who poffefs abundance ; but happy is the man who findeth wifdom,
which is Chrift, the pearl of great price. In him are hid thofe
durable riches and righteoufnefs, the merchandize of which is
better than that of filver, and the gain thereof than fine gold.

TO

TO complain that life has no joys, while there is a single creature whom we can relieve by our bounty, assist by our counsels, or enliven by our presence, is to lament the loss of that which we possess ; and is just as rational as to die of thirst with the cup in our hands.

❖—❧❧❧❧❧❧❧—❖

ENOUGH has Heav'n indulg'd of joy below,
To tempt our tarriance in this lov'd retreat ;
　Enough has Heav'n ordain'd of useful woe,
To make us languish for a happier seat.

YE prou'd, ye selfish, ye severe,
　How vain your mask of state !
The good alone have joy sincere ;
　The good alone are great.

LIFE's road let me cautiously view,
　And no longer disdain to be wise,
Forbearing such paths to pursue,
　As my reason should hate or despise.
To crown both my age and my youth,
　Let me mark where religion has trod,
Since nothing but virtue and truth
　Can reach to the throne of my God.

O DAYS, long lost to man in each degree,
The golden days of hospitality !
When lib'ral fortunes vi'd with lib'ral strife,
To fill the noblest offices of life ;
The poor, at hand their natural patrons saw,
And law-givers were supplements of law !

❖—❧❧❧❧❧❧❧—❖

NEVER treat common beggars with contempt or aversion, though their appearance be ever so offensive ; but remember the kindness of our Saviour and his apostles towards them. Consider, that even they have an equal right with you, to the

　　　　　　　　　　　　protection

protection of Heaven; be thankful that you are not afflicted with their diforders, their fores, or their poverty, but always treat them as your fellow-creatures; for, as they are fuch, it is your duty to wifh them peace of mind in this world, and eternal happinefs in the next; which it is impoffible you can fincerely do, and yet not have the heart to give them a fmall relief.

T H E poor man is, from his fituation, cut off from a thoufand temptations to vice; and that levity and diffipation of thought which are the common attendants of eafe and affluence, are obliged to give way to the fteady exercife of reafon and cool reflection, which are as clofely connected with wifdom, as vice is with folly.

T H E cheft of the mifer might as well contain brafs as gold, unlefs benevolence fhould pour it into the lap of diftrefs, or generofity place it in the hands of merit.

T H E accidents of life are numerous; it is impoffible to guard againft them all; he that meets with the feweft, has a double tie of gratitude to that Being who is about his bed and his paths; he that meets with moft, may convert them into bleffings, by ufing them as means to exalt and improve his virtues. On both fides there is a ftrong call for the exercife of patience and compaffion; and he that exercifes them moft, bears the ftrongeft refemblance to him whofe mercy endureth forever.

W E often overlook the bleffings which are in our poffeffion, to hunt after thofe which are out of our reach.

T R U E greatnefs of foul ought to be conformable to the rules of equity; its object ought to be the doing of all the good it is capable of, without requiring any retribution for the favours granted, or the treafures diftributed.

T E A C H me, oh thou! that teacher art
    Of every duty here below;

The

The number of my days impart;
 Be thou my guide where e'er I go.
I aſk no gold nor length of days,
 I meet thy will, thy will be done;
I know that time itſelf decays,
 And gold but ſparkles in the ſun.
When chaſten'd, let me kiſs the rod;
 I wiſh no tranſient joy to claim;
Be thou my portion, oh, my God!
 'Thro' Heaven's eternal year the ſame.

Extract from an Ode to Senſibility.

NE'ER let my ſoul, with haughty ſcorn,
The prayer of injur'd virtue ſpurn;
Ne'er let my heart, with ſour neglect,
Treat modeſt worth with diſreſpect;
But let my breaſt, like wax receive,
Each fair impreſſion thou canſt give;
Taſte all thy pleaſures, all thy pain,
And pity the unfeeling train!

POOR were the expectations of the ſtudious, the brave, the modeſt and the good, if the reward of their labours and virtues was to be determined by this life.

THAT friendſhip, which makes the leaſt noiſe, is often the moſt uſeful; and a prudent friend, is generally of more ſervice than a zealous one.

THE ſureſt means we can uſe, to arrive at a true eſtimate of ourſelves, and to find out the ſecret faults and vices that lurk within us, is to examine ourſelves by the rules which are laid down for our direction in ſacred hiſtory, and to compare our lives with the life of him who lived up to the perfection of human nature, and is the ſtanding example, as well as the great guide and inſtructor, of thoſe that receive his doctrines.

NO

NO person is infensible to the injury of contempt ; nor is there any talent fo invidious, or fo certain to create ill will, as that of ridicule. The natural effects of years, which all hope to attain, and the infirmities of the body, which none can prevent, are furely of all others the moft improper objects of mirth.

TO receive advice, reproof and inftruction, properly, is the fureft fign of a fincere and humble heart, and fhews a great-nefs of mind, which commands our refpect and reverence, while it appears fo willingly to yield to us the fuperiority.

AVOID the folly of flighting thofe excellencies in others which you have not acquired. Rather endeavour, with a well tempered emulation, to imitate them.

NEVER add confufion to the inquietudes of thofe who have failed of fuccefs in any attempt ; nor exprefs a malicious joy at their difappointment.

WHENE'ER you would an erring friend reprove,
Let gentle cautions fhew the motive's love ;
Do not begin with rafhnefs to exclaim,
But rather hint the fault, before you blame ;
Tis not enough your admonition's juft,
Prudence muft guide it, or the labour's loft ;
Friends fhould affure, and charm us into fenfe,
Harfh counfels lefs reform, than give offence.

A Thought on firft waking.

To God who guards me all the night,
    Be honour, love, and praife ;
To God, who fheds the morning light,
    And gives me length of days.
His pow'r firft call'd us forth from nought,
    Infpir'd the vital flame,
And with amazing wifdom wrought,

The

The whole material frame.
He gave the soul its Heav'nly birth,
    He by his word divine
Prepar'd the fit enclosing earth,
    And bade them both combine.
Strange, that a pure, immortal mind,
    A bright celestial ray,
Should be with frailest nature join'd,
    And mixt with common clay.
O ! wond'rous union, so compos'd,
    That none can understand,
'Tis such as evidently shews
    Th' Almighty Maker's hand.

GREAT inconveniencies attend running into any extremes. Much of our happiness depends upon an evenness of temper, in not suffering the scale of our reason to mount us too high, in the season of prosperity ; nor to sink us too low, with the weight of adversity.

AS whatever worldly substance you enjoy, is, the gift of Providence, make it, in all cases, serve the wise and reasonable ends of a benificent, hospitable life.

WE travel through time, as through a desart of wild and empty wastes, which we would fain hurry over, to get at the imaginary points of rest and pleasure.

IT is a melancholy truth, that though among the talents of our stewardship, Time is the most valuable, yet in general, we are more profuse and regardless of it than of any other.

HAPPY, thrice happy, he whose conscious heart,
Enquires his purpose and discerns his part ;
Who runs, with heed, th' involuntary race,
Nor lets his hours reproach him as they pass;

Weighs

Weighs how they steal away, how sure, how fast,
And as he weighs them, apprehends the last ;
Or vacant, or engag'd, our minutes fly,
We may be negligent, but we must die.

THE lab'ring bee, by God instructed, knows,
Where op'ning flowers their balmy sweets disclose ;
The rising sun, her daily task renews,
Wide, o'er the plains, she sips the pearly dews ;
From mead to mead, she wanders through the skies,
And yellow thyme distends her loaded thighs.
Each rifl'd flow'r rewards her painful toil,
And her full hive receives the golden spoil ;
On flagging wings each load she thither bears,
And while the summer smiles, for winter's wants prepares.

The Ants and the Grashopper.

THE ants, a prudent, painful train,
Brought forth and dri'd their heaps of grain,
A grashopper half starv'd went by,
Who bow'd and beg'd their charity :
To whom a hoary ant reply'd,
In harvest how's your time employ'd?
I sing (the insect said) and play,
To make the lab'ring peasants gay ;
Ah ! cry'd the ant, how just the chance—
As then you sung, you now may dance ;
In vain you here for food apply,
I'll feed no idle folks, not I.

The Fall of the Leaf.

SEE the leaves around ye falling,
    Dry and wither'd to the ground,
Thus to thoughtless mortals calling,
    In a sad and solemn sound.
" Sons of Adam, once in Eden,
    When like us he blighted fell,
Hear the lecture we are reading,

'Tis,

'Tis, alas! the truth we tell.
Virgins much, too much prefuming,
    On your boafted white and red,
View us, late in beauty blooming,
    Number'd now among the dead.
Griping mifers, nightly waking,
    See the end of all your care,
Fled on wings of our own making,
    We have left our owners bare.
Sons of honour, fed on praifes,
    Flutt'ring high in fancied worth,
Lo, the fickle air that raifes,
    Brings us down to parent earth.
Learned fires, in fyftem jaded,
    Who for new ones daily call,
Ceafe, at length, by us perfuaded,
    Every leaf muft have a fall.
Youth, tho' yet no loffes grieve you,
    Gay in health and many a grace,
Let not cloudlefs fkies deceive you,
    Summer gives to autumn place."
On the tree of life eternal,
    Man, let all thy hopes be ftay'd,
Which alone, forever vernal,
    Bears the leaves that never fade.

A MAN who entertains an high opinion of himfelf, is naturally ungrateful. He has too great an efteem of his own merit,
to be thankful for any favours received.

WHEN tired and fick of all mortal vanities, the religious
mind repofes itfelf in the firm expectation of drinking at
the fountain of life, and of bathing in rivers of immortal pleafure; even death (which to the guilty is the gloomy period
of all their joys, and the entrance to a gulph of undying
wretchednefs) brightens into a fmile, and, in an angel's form,
invites the religious foul to endlefs reft from labour, and to endlefs fcenes of joy.

THOU

THOU great, ador'd! thou excellence divine!
Beauty is thine in all its conq'ring pow'rs—
What is there lovely in the fpacious earth,
Or in th' etherial round, compar'd to thee?
In thee we trace up pleafure to hs fource!
Thou art the great original of joy,
Th' eternal fpring of life, the fource of love
Divine—beyond fimilitude fupreme;
With whofe immenfity we're all furrounded!

ACTIVE in indolence, abroad we roam,
In queft of happinefs, which dwells at home;
With vain purfuits fatigu'd, at length we find,
No place excludes it from an equal mind.

OH what a fcene of blifs the foul employs,
Wrapt in the profpeft of eternal joys!
Where all immortal Hallelujahs fing,
And praife the world's Redeemer, Heaven's King;
Where hymns of glory, every voice employ;
Where all is love, and harmony and joy.

A COURSE of virtue, innocence and piety, is fuperior to all the luxury and grandeur, by which the greateft libertines ever propofed to gratify their defires; for then the foul is ftill enlarged, by grafping at the enjoyments of eternal blifs. The mind, by retiring calmly into itfelf, finds there capacities formed for infinite objects and defires, that extend themfelves beyond the limits of this creation, in fearch of the great original of life and pleafure.

SUCH is the uncertainty of human affairs, that we cannot affure ourfelves of the conftant poffeffion of any objects that gratify any one pleafure or defire, except that of virtue; which, as it does not depend on external objects, we may promife ourfelves always to enjoy.

WHEN you are lawfully engaged in the bufinefs of life, take heed that your heart and affections cleave not to the duft.

IT

IT is not without good reason that we are exhorted to pass the time of our sojourning in fear; an attachment to riches, to worldly greatness, or its cares, has a natural tendency to divert the mind from better objects, to draw off its attention from the one thing needful, and to impede its progress in the pursuit of that happiness, which is only worth pursuing.

O WHILE we breathe this fleeting air,
May we for endless life prepare;
To love divine, continue chaste,
All its sweet effluences taste;
'Till at the source, when going hence,
We drink our fill of joy immense!

PROVIDENCE is commonly indulgent to the honest endeavours of industrious persons, that the more laborious they are in their employments, the more they thrive and are blessed in them.

KNOWLEDGE informed with complacency and good breeding, will make a person beloved and admired; but being joined with a severe and morose temper, it makes him rather feared than respected.

WHEN once the soul, by contemplation, is raised to any right apprehension of the divine perfections, and the foretastes of celestial bliss, how will the world, and all that is in it, vanish and disappear before his eyes! With what holy disdain will he look down upon things, which are the highest objects of other men's ambitious desires! All the splendour of courts, all the pageantry of greatness, will no more dazzle his eyes, than the faint lustre of a glow-worm will trouble the eagle after it hath been beholding the sun.

WERE there but a single mercy apportioned to each minute of our lives, the sum would rise very high; but how is our arithmetic confounded, when every minute has more than we can distinctly number!

F   Reflections

Reflections on the Close of the Year.

T H E year expires, and this its lateſt hour——
    Ah think, my ſoul, how ſwift the moment flies,
Nor idly waſte it while it's in thy pow'r ;
    Attend time's awful call, and be thou wiſe.
Twelve months ago, what numbers, blithe and gay,
    Thoughtful, plan'd ſchemes for the ſucceeding year ;
How vain were all their hopes, to death a prey,
    Nor wealth they aſk, nor poverty they fear.
I've follow'd worth and merit to the grave,
    The laſt ſad duties to their aſhes paid ;
How ſoon may I the ſame kind office crave,
    The pitying tear, ſad ſigh and friendly aid ?.
Almighty Lord ! be pleaſed to extend
    Thy wonted kindneſs ; ſtill thy bleſſings pour——
Oh ! may thy grace into my breaſt deſcend,
    Teach me to work thy will, and thee adore.

    O' F all the cauſes which conſpire to blind
Man's erring judgment, and miſguide the mind——
What the weak head, with ſtrongeſt bias rules,
Is PRIDE, the never failing vice of fools.

A R I C H man is no way happier than another man, but that he hath more opportunities miniſtered unto him of doing more good than his neighbour.

H U M I L I T Y is the grand virtue that leads to contentment ; it cuts off the envy and malice of inferiors and equals, and makes us patiently bear the inſults of ſuperiors.

P O V E R T Y has not always the nature of an affliction or judgment, but is rather merely a ſtate of life appointed by providence for the proper trial and exerciſe of the virtues of contentment, patience and reſignation : And for one man to murmur againſt God becauſe he poſſeſſes not thoſe riches he ſees given to another, " is the wrath that killeth the fooliſh man, " and the envy that ſlayeth the ſilly one."   SURELY

S U R E L Y if we did not lose our remembrance, or at least our sensibility, that view would always predominate in our lives, which alone can afford us comfort when we die.

A Serious and contemplative mind sees God in every thing. Every object we behold, the food by which we are sustained, the raiment wherewith we are cloathed, suggest thoughts of piety and gratitude ; and if we attend to the silent voice of meditation, we shall

" Find tongues in trees, books in the running brooks,
" Sermons in stones, and good in every thing."

O U R principles only become pleasing and delightful, when by the influence of them we learn to calm and govern our passions ; and are formed by them into such a temper, as renders us capable of cheerfully enjoying the blessings of the present world, and the higher happiness of a better.

T H E most momentous concern of man, is the state he shall enter upon, after this short and transitory life is ended : And in proportion as eternity is of greater importance than time, so ought men to be solicitous upon what grounds their ex- pectations, with regard to that durable state, are built ; and upon what assurances their hopes or their fears stand.

W E should take all the care imaginable, how we create enemies, it being one of the hardest things in the Christian religion, to behave ourselves as we ought to do towards them.

THE HAPPY MAN.

H A P P Y the man, who free from noisy sports,
And all the pomp and pageantry of courts,
Far from the venal world can live secure,
Be moral, honest, virtuous—tho' poor ;
Who walking still by equity's just rules,
Detesting sordid knaves, and flatt'ring fools ;
Regarding neither fortune, pow'r nor state,

Nor

Nor ever wishing to be vainly great ;
Without malevolence and spleen can live,
And what his neighbour wants, with joy would give ;
A foe to pride, no passion's guilty friend,
Obeying nature, faithful to her end ;
Severe in manners, as in truth severe,
Just to himself, and to his friends sincere ;
His temper even, and his steady mind
Refin'd by friendship, and by books refin'd :
Some low-roof'd cottage holds the happy swain,
Unknown to lux'ry, or her servile train ;
He, studying nature, grows serenely wise,
Like Socrates he lives, or like him dies.
He asks no glory, gain'd by hostile arms,
Nor sighs for grandeur with her painted charms ;
With calm indiff'rence views the shifting scene,
Thro' all magnanimous, resign'd, serene :
On hope sustain'd, he treads life's devious road,
And knows no fear, except the fear of God ;
Would Heav'n, indulgent, grant my fond desire,
Thus would I live, and thus should life expire.

T H E middle state of life is best,
Exalted stations find no rest ;
Storms shake th' aspiring pine and tow'r,
And mountains feel the thunder's pow'r.
The mind, prepar'd for each event,
In every state maintains content ;
She hopes the best when storms prevail,
Nor trusts too far the prosp'rous gale ;
Should time returning winters bring,
Returning winter yields to spring ;
Should darkness shroud the present skies,
Hereafter brighter suns shall rise.

A WISE Heathen was of opinion, that if mankind, in general, had the power given them to change their station in life, and at the same time were made acquainted with the inconveniencies niences attending every other ftate, as well as their own, they would unanimoufly choofe to continue in the fituation they were at firft placed in by Providence.

THE firft ingredient in converfation is truth; the next good fenfe; the third good humour; the laft wit.

DISCREET people generally have a referve of neceffaries before-hand, that when the time comes for ufing them, there may be no hurry and confufion.

CIVILITY overacted, is always fufpicious. A blaft of thorns begins in a blaze, and foon ends in a fmoke; but a fire made of proper materials, defigned to be ufeful and lafting, at its firft kindling breaks out from a cloud of fmoke, and grows clearer and brighter as it burns.

PLUTARCH (in his book of friendfhip) directs us, to " make a trial of our friends, as of our money, and to be equally cautious of choofing both." Tacitus tells us, that " the longer a friendfhip is contracted, fo much the furer and more firm it is." From this we may collect, that an old friend is always to be moft valued, the beft to be loved, and the firft to be trufted.

THE duties that are owing to friends, are integrity, love, counfel and affiftance. It is not intimacy, and frequency of converfation, that makes a friend, but a difinterefted obfervance of thefe duties.

NEVER admit (fays the philofopher Seneca) vain glory into your heart; for human glory is at beft no more than human folly.

THE pleafing gales that gentle fummer yields,
   Amid the gay profufion of his ftore;
The fmiles of nature, and of verdant fields,
   Are all, alas! but bleffings of an hour.

How

How vaſt the beauties they around diſplay,
   Till dreary winter reaſſumes his reign,
And ſternly bids them vaniſh and decay,
   And leave no traces on the penſive plain.
The golden cowſlip on th' enamell'd mead,
   Diſplays his youthful glories to the view,
But ſoon he droops his ſolitary head,
   And yields his virtue to the evening's dew.
Alas! how tranſient is the dream of life,
   And every heart-felt comfort we enjoy;
And fraught with care, ſolicitude and ſtrife,
   Each hour attempts our bleſſings to deſtroy.
All human ſcenes are ſubject to decay,
   And time aſſerts an all-prevailing pow'r;
Expanding beauties to the morning's ray,
   We bloom to wither, as the tender flow'r.
Not ſo the ſoul—its views ſublime and pure,
   Where faith, and hope, and charity unite,
Shall riſe, and dwell eternally ſecure,
   In Heaven's unfading manſions of delight.

MERE baſhfulneſs, without merit, is awkward; and merit, without modeſty, inſolent: But modeſt merit has a double claim to acceptance, and generally meets with as many patrons as beholders.

XENOPHON in his Cyrus, which he deſigned for the perfect idea of a good prince, repreſents him in the laſt minutes of his life, addreſſing himſelf to God to this purpoſe: "Thou "knoweſt that I have been a lover of mankind; and now that "I am leaving this world, I hope to find that mercy from "thee which I have ſhewn to others."

THE man who keeps the golden mean
Where raging ſtorms are ſeldom ſeen,
Avoids the dang'rous rocks and pools,
That fright the wiſe, and ſwallow fools.

                                             THE

T H E limits of our life, how like a shade—
A passing cloud—our vain existence flies !
Yet all our boundless hopes, our future views,
For endless ages, on this narrow span,
This little rivulet of time, depend.
And Oh ! how fast the gliding current flows !
Nothing retards its everlasting course ;
Ev'n now our hasty moments pass away,
Forever, O forever are they gone !
We die with every breath ; no calling back
The nicest point of all our vain duration ;
'Tis past beyond retrieve !————but Oh ! there rest
Eternal things on this important point :
This span of life, this short allotted span,
Is all we have to manage for the stake
Of an immortal soul ; the glorious weight
Of Heav'nly crowns and kingdoms are suspended,
And Oh !—if lost, can never be recall'd !

W H A T impression can treasure and great possessions make
upon the mind that is contemplating, seriously, on the kingdom of Heaven, and a crown of glory that never fades away ?
What are the pomp and majesty of an earthly court ; the mag-
nificence of palaces and crouded theatres, to one who has in
view the glories of Heaven ; the triumphs of the saints ; and
the ineffable splendour of the angelic order ? What are feasts,
sports, plays, and all the varieties of sensual pleasures and delights, to him who stedfastly fixes his eye on celestial bliss, and
everlasting transports of joy ?

H E that would pass the latter part of life with honour and
decency, must, when he is young, consider that he shall one
day be old, and lay up knowledge for his support, when his
powers of acting shall forsake him ; and remember when he is
old, that he has once been young, and forbear to animadvert,
with unnecessary rigour, on faults which experience only can
correct.

Written

Written in the Holy Bible.

YE facred tomes, be my unerring guide,
Dove-hearted faints, and prophets eagle-ey'd !
I fcorn the moral fop and ethic fage,
But drink in truth from your illumin'd page :
Like Mofes' bufh, each leaf's divinely bright,
Where God invefts himfelf in milder light ;
Taught by your doctrines we devoutly rife,
Faith points the way, and hope unbars the fkies.
You tune our paffions, teach them how to roll,
And fink the body but to raife the foul ;
To raife it, bear it to myfterious day,
Nor want an angel to direct the way !

TO THE MOTHER.

SAY, while you prefs, with growing love,
   The darling to your breaft,
And all a mother's pleafures prove,
   Are you entirely bleft ?
Ah ! no ; a thoufand tender cares,
   By turns your thoughts employ ;
Now rifing hopes, now anxious fears,
   And grief fucceeds to joy.
Dear innocent, her lovely fmiles,
   With what delight you view !
But ev'ry pain the infant feels,
   The mother feels it too.
Then whifpers bufy, cruel fear,
   " The child, alas, may die !"
And nature prompts the ready tear,
   And heaves the rifing figh.
Say, does not Heav'n our comforts mix
   With more than equal pain,
To teach us, if our hearts we fix
   On earth we fix in vain ?
Then be our earthly joys refign'd,
   Since here we cannot reft ;
For earthly joys were ne'er defign'd
   To make us fully bleft.

PATIENCE

PATIENCE confifts in a well pleafed fubmiffion to the divine will, and a quiet yielding to whatever it pleafes the Deity to afflict us with. If we are poffeffed with a fincere reverence and efteem of God, humility will fortify us with patience to fuffer, and not murmur, at his difpenfations.

IN every affair of life, defpair fhould give way to hope, and impatience to content; for the hand of Providence is always neareft to affift us, when perils are moft evident.

AFFLICTIONS, if we make a difcreet ufe of them, are meffengers of love from Heaven to invite us thither.

A SOUL immortal, fpending all her fires,
Wafting her ftrength in ftrenuous idlenefs,
Thrown into tumult, raptur'd or alarm'd,
At aught this fcene can threaten or indulge,
Refembles ocean into tempeft wrought,
To waft a feather, or to drown a fly.

The Knowledge of God natural to Man.

THAT gracious Pow'r, who, from his kindred clay,
Bids man arife to tread the realms of day,
Implants a guide, that tells what will fulfil
His word, or what's repugnant to his will;
The author of our being marks fo clear,
That none, but thofe who will be blind, can err;
Or wherefoe'er we turn th' attentive eyes,
Proofs of a God on ev'ry fide arife;
Nature, a faithful mirror, ftands to fhew
God, in his works, difclos'd to human view;
Whate'er exifts beneath the chryftal floods,
Or cuts the liquid air, or haunts the woods;
The various flow'rs, that fpread th' enamell'd mead,
Each plant, each herb, or ev'n the grafs we tread,
Difplays Omnipotence: None elfe could form
The vileft weed, or animate a worm.

Or

Or view the livid wonders of the ſky,
What hand ſuſpends thoſe pond'rous orbs on high?
The comets flight, the planets myſtic dance!
Are theſe the works of Providence or chance?
Themſelves declare that univerſal cauſe
Who fram'd the ſyſtem, and impos'd their laws.

CHRISTIANITY is not a ſpeculative ſcience, but a practical obligation.

PIETY and pride can no more thrive together, than health and ſickneſs, light and darkneſs.

THO' our nature is imperfect and corrupt, yet it is ſo far improvable, by the grace of God upon our own good endeavours, that we all may, tho' not equally, be inſtruments of his glory, ornaments and bleſſings to this world, and capable of eternal happineſs.

THERE is a certain candour in true virtue, which none can counterfeit.

IN the moderate uſe of lawful things, there can be no crime; but in all extremes there is.

" WE cannot (ſays Amaſis in his epiſtle to Polycartes) ex-
" pect in this world an unmixt happineſs, without being fre-
" quently tempered with troubles and diſaſters."

THE family is the proper province for private women to ſhine in.

TEMPERANCE is a regimen into which all perſons may put themſelves.

GOD hath promiſed pardon to him that repenteth; but he hath not promiſed repentance to him that ſinneth.

HEAV'N's

HEAV'N's favours here are trials, not rewards;
A call to duty, not discharge from care,
And should alarm us full as much as woes;
Awake us to their cause and consequence,
O'er our scan'd conduct give a jealous eye,
And make us tremble, weigh'd with our desert.

TO man's false optics (from his folly false)
Time, in advance, behind him hides his wings,
And seems to creep, decrepid with his age;
Behold him when pass'd by! what then is seen
But his broad pinions swifter than the winds?
And all mankind, in contradiction strong,
Rueful, aghast! cry out at his career.

A DREAM.

TORTUR'D with pain, as late I sleepless lay,
Opprefs'd with care, impatient for the day,
Just at the dawn, a gentle slumber came,
And to my wand'ring fancy brought this dream.
Methought my pains were hush'd, and I was laid
In earth's cold lap, among the silent dead;
Prop'd on my arm, I view'd, with vast surprize, ⎫
This last retreat of all the great and wise; ⎬
Where fool, with knave, in friendly consort lies. ⎭
Whilst thus I gaz'd, behold a wretch appear'd,
In beggar's garb, with loathsome filth besmear'd,
His carcase, Lazar like, was crusted o'er
With odious leprosy, one horrid sore;
This wretch approach'd, and laid him by my side,
Good Heaven!—how great a shock to mortal pride;
Enrag'd I cry'd—" friend, keep the distance due
" To us of rank, from beggars such as you;
" Observe some manners, and do me the grace,
" To move far off, and quit your betters place."
   " And what art thou? audacious (he reply'd!)
" That thus dost shew such reliques of thy pride?
" What tho' in life the harder lot was mine,
" Of ease and plenty every blessing thine,
                                          " Yet

" Yet here, diſtinctions ceaſe ; a beggars duſt
" Shall riſe with kings—more happy if more juſt ;
" Till then we both one common maſs ſhall join,
" And ſpite of ſcorn, my aſhes mix with thine."

ON WRITING.

BLESS'D be the man, his memory at leaſt,
That found the art, thus to unfold his breaſt,
And taught ſucceeding times an eaſy way,
Their ſecret thoughts by letters to convey ;
To baffle abſence, and ſecure delight,
Which, till that time, was limited to ſight ;
The parting farewel ſpoke the laſt adieu,
The leſs'ning diſtance paſt, then loſs of view ;
The friend was gone, which ſome kind moments gave,
And abſence ſeparated like the grave.
When for a wife the youthful Patriarch ſent,
The camels, jewels, and a ſervant went,
And wealthy equipage, tho' grave and ſlow,
But not a line that might the lover ſhew.
The rings and bracelets woo'd her hands and arms ;
But had ſhe known of melting words the charms,
That under ſecret ſeals in ambuſh lie,
To catch the ſoul when drawn into the eye,
The fair Aſſyrian had not took his guide,
Nor her ſoft heart in chains of hair been ti'd.

WERE it lawful and becoming in man to chooſe his circumſtances in life, a mediocrity would perhaps be the moſt
uſeful, and the freeſt from temptation ; though notwithſtand-
ing theſe advantages, ſome might think it not the moſt deſir-
able. Opulence may tempt us to diſſipation, indolence, ſen-
ſuality, and total forgetfulneſs of God ; poverty, to envy,
falſhood, diſhoneſty and perjury. Let us, therefore, ſay with
Agur, " Give me neither poverty nor riches, feed me with
" food convenient for me ; leſt I be full and deny thee, and
" ſay, who is the Lord ? or be poor and ſteal, and take the
" name

" name of my God in vain." But even thofe Chriftians, who move in this middle fphere, have their forrows and their joys; they feel fome degree of pain, fome proportionable meafure of anxiety and care; they tafte a bitter mixed with every fweet, and they find a faithful monitor within, who tells them that the earth is not their portion, was not given as their reft, nor intended as their home.

MY God, the fteps of pious men
  Are order'd by thy will;
Tho' they fhould fall, they rife again,
  Thy hand fupports them ftill.
I choofe the path of Heav'nly truth,
  And glory in my choice;
Not all the riches of the earth
  Could make me fo rejoice.

To Mira, on removing into the Country.

MIRA, while on earth we ftay,
Change our refidence we may;
Change it often, and yet ftill
May be happy if wè will.
Virtue ftill fhall be our care,
The Deity is every where;
Every where to blefs the good,
Seen, tho' little underftood.
Seen his wifdom, goodnefs, pow'r,
When we cultivate the flow'r;
Wifdom all its hues difclofe,
Its perfume with goodnefs glows;
Finite pow'rs in Heav'n or earth
Cou'd not give the charmer birth.
  God fhall fend our board to fpread
Healthful herbage from the bed;
Cooling fruit from every bough,
Milk and butter from the cow
From the hive the comb replete,
Such was Ifrael's Canaan treat;

G

Chicks

Chicks that once before our door .
Pick'd the crumbs and aſk'd for more ;
Pigs that grunted in our ſty,
Lambs that ſkip'd when we were by ;
This is goodneſs in exceſs,
Oh ! how Heav'n delights to. bleſs.
From the vine the gen'rous juice,
Not for luxury but uſe,
Pour'd for Mira, pour'd for me—
If content, how happy we.
    Whereſoe'er we turn our eyes,
How the varying proſpects riſe !
Fertiliz'd by ſun and rain,
Earth how cloath'd with graſs and grain ;
Groves with muſick fill our ears,
How the God, the God! appears ;
He o'er barren hill and dale
Bade the farmers toil avail ;
Gave the linnet's note refin'd,
With its joys to charm mankind.
Mira, what ſo clear as this,
Joy in others gives us bliſs ?
With our ſuperfluous ſtore
Let us clothe and feed the poor.
Worth that from the public flies,
Let us ſeek and patronize ;
Worth that hopes for no diſplay,
'Till that all diſcloſing day ;
Mira! then may you and I,
Claim a manſion in the ſky.

FORTITUDE has its extremes, as well as the reſt of the virtues ; and ought, like them, to be always attended by prudence.

THE end of learning is, to know God, and out of that knowledge, to love him, and to imitate him, as we may the neareſt, by poſſeſſing our ſouls of true virtue.

CICERO

CICERO says, " Vicious habits are so great a stain to
" human nature, and so odious in themselves, that every person
" actuated by right reason, would avoid them, though he was
" sure they would be always concealed both from God and
" man, and had no future punishment entailed upon them."

AS to be perfectly just, is an atribute of the divine nature ;
to be so to the utmost of our abilities, is the glory of a man.

A VIRTUOUS habit of mind is so absolutely necessary to
influence the whole life, and beautify every particular action ;
to overbalance or repel all the gilded charms of avarice, pride,
and self-interest, that a man deservedly procures the lasting epi-
thets of good or bad, as he appears either swayed by, or regardless of it.

A MAN of virtue is an honour to his country, a glory to
humanity, a satisfaction to himself, and a benefactor to the
world. He is rich without oppression or dishonesty, charitable without ostentation, courteous without deceit, and brave
without vice.

ANGER may glance into the breast of a wise man, but
rests only in the bosom of fools.

WHEN the last hour seems to be approaching, all terrestrial advantages are viewed with indifference ; and the value
that we once set upon them, is disregarded or forgotten. And
if the same thought was always predominant, we should then
find the absurdity of stretching out our arms incessantly to
grasp that which we cannot keep ; and wearing out ourselves
in endeavours to add new turrets to the fabric of ambition,
when the foundation itself is shaking, and the ground on which
it stands is mouldering away.

TO him who is animated with a view of obtaining approbation from the Sovereign of the universe, no difficulty should
seem insurmountable.

WE have seen those virtues which have, while living, retired from the public eye, generally transmitted to posterity, as
the truest objects of admiration and praise.　　　　A

A Hymn.—Pſalm VIIIth.

LORD! how illuſtrious is thy name,
Whoſe pow'r both Heav'n and earth proclaim!
When I the Heav'ns, thy fabric, ſee,
The moon and ſtars, diſpos'd by thee;
O! what is man, or his frail race,
That thou ſhould'ſt ſuch a ſhadow grace?
Next to thy angels moſt renown'd,
With majeſty and glory crown'd?
All that on dales and mountains feed,
All that the woods and deſarts breed,
Whate'er thro' airy regions flees,
Or ſwims in deep and ſtormy ſeas,
Thou all beneath his feet haſt laid,
King of thy whole creation made;
Lord! how illuſtrious is thy name,
Whoſe pow'r both Heav'n and earth proclaim.

I ENVY no one's birth or ſ
　　Their title, train or dreſs;
Nor has my pride e'er ſtretch'd its aim,
　　Beyond what I poſſeſs.
I aſk not, wiſh not, to appear,
　　More beauteous, rich or gay;
Lord make me wiſer every year,
　　And better every day.

A WISE and virtuous man can never be proud; nor can
he be exalted in his thoughts at any advantages he has above
others, becauſe he is conſcious of his own weakneſs and inabili-
ty to become either wiſe or virtuous, by any thing he finds in
his own power; and his ſenſe of the goodneſs of the bountiful
God in beſtowing upon him more abundantly, what he has
been pleaſed more ſparingly to vouchſafe to others, will inſpire his ſoul with humility, thankfulneſs and adoration.

MEN

MEN generally love to have their praises proclaimed, not whispered. There are not many who can have the patience to stay till the day of judgment, to receive the approbation and applause of their good actions.

- - - - - - - - - - -

Verses written on the Severity of Winter.

WHILE the fierce winter rages all around,
And the hard earth's with frosty fetters bound ;
While clothes its surface a thin garb of snow,
And rapid rivers now no longer flow :
Tho' keen the piercing cold, the vital flood,
The rich can warm with raiment, fire and food ;
But whence the poor enable to sustain
Oppressive want, and hunger's urgent pain ?
How is it, naked, hungry—they can bear,
In their defenceless state, the piercing air ?
Whence shall the wretch the just supply receive ?
Ought man refuse, when God empow'rs to give ?
None can—but those in whom compassion fails ;
In whom nor love of God nor man prevails ;
In whom all serious sense of duty's lost,
Colder their hearts than snow, and harder than the frost.

- - - - - - - - - - -

ALL have their frailties. Whoever looks for a friend without imperfections, will never find what he seeks ; we love ourselves with all our faults, and we ought to love our friend in like manner.

THERE is nothing so engaging as a benevolent disposition. This temper makes a man's behaviour inoffensive, affable and obliging ; it multiplies friends, and disarms the malice of an enemy.

A MAN without complaisance, ought to have a great deal of merit in the room of it.

HE

H E whofe honeft freedom makes it his virtue to
what he thinks, makes it his neceffity to think what is

HYMN for the MORNING.

O N thee, each morning, O my God!
  My waking thoughts attend,
In whom are founded all my hopes,
  And all my wifhes end.
My foul, in pleafing wonder loft,
  Thy boundlefs love furveys,
And, fir'd with grateful zeal, prepares,
  Her facrifice of praife.
Thou lead'ft me thro' the maze of fleep,
  And bring'ft me fafe to light,
And with the fame paternal care,
  Conduct'ft my fteps till night.
When ev'ning flumbers prefs mine eyes,
  With thy protection bleft,
In peace and fafety I commit
  My wearied limbs to reft.
My fpirit, in thy hand fecure,
  Fears no approaching ill;
For, whether waking or afleep,
  Thou, Lord! art with me ftill.
What fit return can I, weak flefh,
  Make to Almighty Pow'r!
For fo much goodnefs, fo much love!
  Such mercies every hour!
I'll daily, to th' aftonifh'd world,
  His wond'rous acts proclaim,
Whilft all with me fhall praifes fing,
  With me fhall blefs his name.
At morn, at noon, at night, I'll ftill,
  The growing work purfue;
And him alone will praife, to whom
  Alone all praife is due.

I T is a fign of great prudence, to be willing to receive inftruction; the moft intelligent perfon, fometimes, ftands in need of it.

THERE is nothing more difagreeable, than continual jefting. By endeavouring to purchafe the reputation of being pleafant, a man lofes the advantage of being thought wife.

I T is ungenerous to give a perfon occafion to blufh at his own ignorance in any one thing, who perhaps may excel us in many.

THE greateft wifdom of fpeech, is to know when, and what, and where to fpeak; the time, matter and manner. The next to it, is filence.

A S we fhould never conftrue that in earneft, which is fpoken in jeft, fo we fhould not fpeak that in jeft, which may be eonftrued in earneft.

T H E talent of turning men into ridicule, and expofing thofe we converfe with, is the qualification of little, ungenerous tempers. What an abfurd thing it is to pafs over all the valuable parts of a man, and fix our attention on his infirmities; to obferve his imperfections more than his virtues!

A S, amongft wife men, he is the wifeft who thinks he knows leaft, fo, amongft fools, he is the greateft who thinks he knows moft.

THERE is far more fatisfaction in doing, than receiving good. To relieve the oppreffed, is the moft glorious act a man is capable of; it is in fome meafure doing the bufinefs of God and Providence; and is attended with a Heavenly pleafure, unknown but to thofe that are beneficent and liberal.

L E T worldly minds the world purfue,
It has no charms for me;

Once

Once I admir'd its trifles too,
   But grace has set me free.
Its pleasures now no longer please,
   No more content afford,
Far from my heart be joys like these,
   Now I have known the Lord.
As by the light of op'ning day,
   The stars are all conceal'd;
So earthly pleasures fade away,
   When Jesus is reveal'd.
Now, Lord! I would be thine alone,
   And wholly live to thee;
But may I hope that thou wilt own
   A worthless worm like me?
Yes—tho' of sinners I'm the worst,
   I cannot doubt thy will;
For if thou had'st not lov'd me first
   I had refus'd thee still.

ALPHONSUS, king of Sicily, being asked what he would reserve for himself, who gave so much away? Even those things, said he, that I do give, for the rest I esteem as nothing.

NO character is more attractive of universal respect, than that of helping those who are in no condition of helping themselves.

THE temperate man's pleasures are durable, because they are regular; and all his life is calm and serene, because it is innocent.

SOCRATES said, "all the treasures of the earth " were not to be compared to the least virtue of the soul."

THE gifts of the mind are able to cover the defects of the body; but the perfections of the body cannot hide the imperfections of the mind.

THOUGH

THOUGH prudence may oblige a man to fecure a competency, yet never was any one by right reafon induced to feek fuperfluities.

RICHNESS of drefs contributes nothing to a man of fenfe, but rather makes his fenfe enquired into. The more the body is fet off, the mind appears the lefs.

THE greateft pleafure wealth can afford us, is that of doing good.

OF all the things this world affords us, the poffeffion and enjoyment of wifdom alone is immortal. A ftrict adherence to virtue, and a well regulated life, renders our pleafures more folid and lafting.

IF we apply ourfelves ferioufly to wifdom, we fhall never live without true pleafure, but learn to be pleafed with every thing. We fhall be pleafed fo far with wealth, as it makes us beneficial to others; with poverty, for not having much to care for; and with obfcurity, for being unenvied.

The Angler and the Philofopher.

BESIDE a gentle murm'ring brook,
   An angler took his patient ftand,
He ey'd the ftream with anxious look,
   And wav'd his rod with cautious hand.
The bait with niceft art was dreft,
   The fifhes left their fafe retreat,
And one more eager than the reft,
   Look'd, long'd, and fwallow'd the deceit.
Too late fhe felt the poignant fmart,
   Her pitying friends her fate deplore,
The angler, with well-practic'd art,
   Hook'd, play'd, and drew her to the fhore.
Lur'd by the beauty of the day,
   The fun now finking in the fky.

A

A sage pursu'd his walk that way,
 And saw the bleeding victim lie.
Far in the vale of years declin'd,
 He watch'd the course of nature's law ;
And thus with philosophic mind,
 He moraliz'd on what he saw.
Indulge, a while, the pensive vein,
 Aud fix this image in your mind,
You've hook'd a fish—observe its pain,
 And view the state of human kind.
Fate gives us line, we shift the scene,
 And jocund, traverse to and fro,
Pain, sickness, still will intervene,
 We feel the hook where e'er we go.
If proudly, we our schemes extend,
 And look beyond the present hour,
We find our straiten'd prospects end,
 And own an over-ruling pow'r.
Awhile we sport, awhile lament,
 Fate checks the line and we are gone ;
Dragg'd from our wonted element
 To distant climes, untry'd, unknown.

***

IT is no common blessing to meet with a faithful, sensible, and discreet friend ; faithful to conceal nothing from us ; sensible to remark our faults ; and discreet to reprehend us for them. But to be able to believe and follow his advice, is indeed a real happiness. It frequently happens, that we take a pride in following our own conceits ; like those travellers that lose their way for want of taking a guide, or enquiring after the road.

SLANDER is the revenge of a coward, and dissimulation his defence.

***

BEWARE what earth calls happiness ; beware
All joys, but joys that never can expire ;   Who

Who builds on lefs than an immortal bafe,
Fond as he feems, condemns his joys to death.

Infcription over the Door of a Gentleman's Retreat:

BENEATH this mofs-grown roof, within this cell,
Truth, liberty, content and virtue dwell;
Say you who dare, this happy place difdain,
What fplendid palace boafts fo fair a train?

VIRTUE's the friend of life, the foul of health,
The poor man's comfort, and the rich man's wealth.

IT is not fufficient, that the Chriftian avoid only the com-
miffion of known actual fins; for more is certainly required
of him who is commanded to abftain from all appearance of
evil; who is to fpeak the truth to his neighbour, and fo to
walk that he may be pronounced blamelefs and without re-
buke in the midft of this crooked and perverfe generation.
Circumfpection in the ordering of our fpeech, is, in fome re-
fpects, perhaps, as neceffary for the ornament of religion, as the
outward deportment of our conduct in the world; or, at leaft,
as neceffary for the approbation of him, who, as one expreffes,
" Views effects in their caufes, and actions in their motives;"
or, to ufe words ftill more awful, who hath declared, that
" Every idle word which men fhall fpeak, they fhall give an
" account thereof in the day of judgment."

DISCRETION does not only fhew itfelf in words, but
in all the circumftances of action, and is like an under agent
of Providence, to guide and direct us in the ordinary concerns
of life.

IMPRINT this maxim deeply in your mind, that there is
nothing certain in this human and mortal ftate; by which
means you will avoid being tranfported with profperity, and
being dejected in adverfity.

O!

O! BORN for nobler ends! dare to be wife;
'Tis not e'en now too late, affert thy claim;
Rugged the path conducting to the fkies,
But the fair prize is an immortal fame.

<hr/>

HOUSHOLD affairs ought infenfibly to flide along,
and reprefent a ftill current without noife or waves.

CLEARNESS is the rule of fpeaking, as fincerity is the rule
of thinking. Too bright fallies of wit, like flafhes of lightning,
rather dazzle than illuminate.

LESSONS and precepts ought to be gilded and fweetened
as we do pills and potions, fo as to take off the difguft of the
remedy ; for it holds both in virtue and in health, that we love
to be inftructed, as well as phyfick'd with pleafure.

<hr/>

Verfes fent to a young Woman, with a Carnation growing in
a Flower-Pot.

WHILE this gay flower attracts thy eager fight,
And gives to every feeling fenfe delight,
Let its beft ufe thy better thoughts employ,
And yield thee profit, while it gives thee joy.
Like thee in beauty's faireft noon it blows,
Flames as the fun, and as the ruby glows ;
But time, that fixes every mortal's fate,
Marks its fhort exit, and uncertain date.
Thus the bright charms of youth and love decay,
As the fine flower that fcents a fummer's day ;
Soon will the fpoils of time thy mind engage,
And e'en thy beauty wither into age ;
Amid the frolics of engaging youth,
Be thine the care to hoard the charms of truth ;
To mark the moment fancy's pow'rs decay,
And place thy blifs beyond the fleeting day.

A

A TREE that is every year tranfplanted, will never bear fruit ; and a mind that is always hurried from its proper ftation, will fcarce ever do good in any.

SUPPOSING men were to live forever in this world, it would be hardly poffible for them to do more towards their eftablifhment here, than they now do.

LIBERALITY fhould have fuch a mixture of prudence, as not to exceed the ability of the giver.

WITH a falfe companion, it is hard to retain innocence ; be, therefore, very cautious in choofing your company.

RESOLVE to fpeak and act well in company, in oppofition to thofe that do ill ; whofe vice fet againft thy virtue, will render it the more confpicuous and excellent.

An Elegy written when the Bells were tolling for the Interment of a Corpfe.

HARK! now the folemn peal begins,
 And founds the fad alarm ;
Forfake, it cries, forfake your fins,
 And fhun impending harm.
Behold ! the corpfe approaching near,
 View there your tranfient ftate ;
Beftow at leaft one pious tear,
 And with fubmiffion wait.
'Ere long this melancholy fcene,
 Shall on your hearfe attend ;
With hafte employ the fpace between,
 To make of God your friend.
Then fhall your mind feel fweet repofe,
 Nor care difturb your reft,
Virtue alone this peace beftows,
 And thus rewards the bleft.

H   SLIGHT

SLIGHT not those joys Heaven's bounty doth bestow,
Pursuing what was never found below ;
So many ills in stormy life abound,
" In Heaven alone true happiness is found."

The Close of the Year.

AS rapid rolls the year away,
    Down the swift current of the times,
A moment let the reader stay,
    And mark the moral of my rhymes.
As rivers glide towards the sea,
    And sink and lose them in the main,
So man declines—and what is he ?
    His hope, his wish; alas, how vain !
Fast goes the year , but still renew'd,
    The ball of time knows no decay ;
Sure signal of that greatest good,
    We hope in God's eternal day.

YOUR wit may make clear things doubtful ; but it is your prudence to make doubtful things clear.

IN conversation, a man of good sense will seem to be less knowing, to be more obliging, and choose to be on a level with others, rather than oppress with the superiority of his genius.

IT is according to nature, to be merciful ; for no man that hath not divested himself of humanity, can be hard-hearted to others, without feeling a pain in himself.

TRUE honour, as defined by Cicero, is the concurrent approbation of good men ; such only being fit to give true praise, who are themselves praise-worthy.

NOBILITY is to be considered only as an imaginary distinction, unless accompanied with the practice of those generous virtues by which it ought to be obtained. Titles of honour, conferred upon such as have no personal merit to deserve them, are at best but the royal stamp set upon base metal.   TO

TO PEACE.

COME, lovely, gentle, peace of mind,
  With all thy smiling nymphs around,
Content and innocence combin'd,
  With wreath of sacred olive crown'd.
Come, thou that lov'st the walk at eve,
  · The banks of murm'ring streams along,
That lov'st the crowded court to leave,
  And hear the milk-maid's simple song ;
That lov'st, with contemplation's eye,
  The head-long cataract to view,
That foams and thunders from on high,
  While echoes oft the sound renew ;
That lov'st the dark sequester'd wood,
  Where silence spreads her brooding wings,
Nor less the lake's translucent flood,
  The mossy grots and bubbling springs.
With thee, the lamp of wisdom burns,
  The guiding light to realms above ;
With thee, the raptur'd mortal learns
  The wonders of celestial love.
With thee, the poor have endless wealth,
  And sacred freedom glads the slave ;
With thee, the sick rejoice in health, · ▪
  The weak are strong, the fearful brave.
O lovely, gentle peace of mind,
  Be thou on earth my constant guest ;
With thee, whate'er in life I find,
  This pledge of Heav'n shall make me blest.

AS no man lives so happy, but to some his life would seem unpleasant ; so we find none so miserable, but one shall hear of another that would change calamities with him.

HE that is ashamed to be seen in a mean condition, would probably be proud of a splendid one.

IMPRINT

IMPRINT this maxim deeply in your mind, that there is nothing certain in this human and mortal state ; by which means you will avoid being transported with prosperity, and being dejected in adversity.

ENDEAVOUR to make peace among thy neighbours. It is a worthy and reputable action, and will bring greater and juster commendations to thee, and more benefit to those with whom thou conversest, than wit or learning, or any of those so much admired accomplishments.

PREFER solid sense to wit ; never study to be diverting, without being useful ; let no jest intrude upon good manners, nor say any thing that may offend modesty.

BE slow in choosing a friend, and slower to change him ; courteous to all ; intimate with few. Slight no man for his meanness, nor esteem any for their wealth and greatness alone.

AN idle body is a kind of monster in the creation. All nature is busy about him. How wretched is it to hear people complain, that the day hangs heavy upon them ; that they do not know what to do with themselves. How absurd are such expressions among creatures, who can apply themselves to the duties of religion and meditation ; to the reading of useful books ; who may exercise themselves in the pursuits of knowledge and virtue, and every hour of their lives make themselves wiser and better than they were before.

A Contemplation on Night.

WHETHER amid the gloom of night I stray,
Or my glad eyes enjoy revolving day,
Still nature's various face informs my sense
Of an all-wise, all-powerful Providence.
When the gay sun first breaks the shades of night,
And strikes the distant hills with eastern light,

Colour

Colour returns, the plains their liv'ry wear,
And a bright verdure clothes the smiling year ;
The blooming flowers with opening beauties glow,
And grazing flocks their milky fleeces shew.
The barren cliffs, with chalky fronts, arise,
And a pure azure arches o'er the skies.
But when the gloomy reign of night returns,
Stript of her fading pride, all nature mourns ;
The trees no more their wonted verdure boast,
But weep, in dewy tears, their beauty lost.
No distant landskips draw our curious eyes,
Wrapt in night's robe the whole creation lies.
Yet still ev'n now, while darkness clothes the land,
We view the traces of th' Almighty hand ;
Millions of stars in Heaven's wide vault appear,
And with new glories hang the boundless sphere.
The silver moon her western couch forsakes,
And o'er the skies her nightly circle makes ;
Her solid globe beats back the sunny rays,
And to the world her borrow'd light repays.
    Whether those stars that twinkling lustre send
Are suns, and rolling worlds those suns attend,
Man may conjecture, and new schemes declare,
Yet all his systems but conjectures are.
But this we know, that Heaven's eternal king,
Who bid this universe from nothing spring,
Can at his word bid num'rous worlds appear,
And rising worlds th' all-powerful word shall hear.
    When to the western main the sun descends,
To other lands a rising day he lends ;
The spreading dawn another shepherd spies,
The wakeful flocks from their warm folds arise.
Refresh'd, the peasant seeks his early toil,
And bids the plow correct the fallow soil ;
While we, in sleep's embraces, waste the night,
The climes oppos'd enjoy meridian light.
And when those lands the busy sun forsakes,
With us again the rosy morning wakes ;
In lazy sleep the night rolls swift away,
And neither clime laments his absent ray.

When

When the pure foul is from the body flown,
No more fhall night's alternate reign be known;
The fun no more fhall rolling light beſtow,
But from th' Almighty ſtreams of glory flow.
Oh! may ſome nobler thought my ſoul employ,
Than empty, tranſient, ſublunary joy!
The ſtars fhall drop, the fun ſhall loſe his flame,
But thou, O God! forever ſhine the ſame.

A S riches are in general the means of procuring ſome of the comforts, and almoſt all the conveniencies of life, we moſt commonly think that happineſs is annexed to the poſſeſſion of them. We, therefore, toil and labour for abundance; and when abundance is obtained, we find as many wants, as many cares, and as many ſorrows, as when humble poverty was our only burthen; when induſtry procured the neceſſaries of life; or when mediocrity of circumſtances placed us beyond the reach of want.

I T is our buſineſs to follow the leadings of Divine Providence, as the beſt and wiſeſt rule for our conduct in every ſtage and circumſtance of life. If worldly affluence is to be the portion of the labouring man, the hand of God will point out the way, and he will ſurmount the greateſt difficulties.

L E T us be particularly careful to ſhun all occaſion of ſuperfluous diſcourſe, and watch over our words, that we utter nothing but what may tend to the glory of God, or the good of our neighbour.

H E that does good for virtue's ſake, ſeeks neither praiſe nor reward, though ſure of both at laſt.

T H I S fib'rous frame, by nature's kindly law,
Which gives each joy to keen ſenſation here,
O'er purer ſcenes of bliſs the veil may draw,
And cloud reflection's more exalted ſphere.   When

When death's cold hand, with all-diffolving pow'r,
  Shall the clofe tie with friendly ftroke unbind,
Alike our mortal as our natal hour
  May to new being wake the rifing mind ;
On death's new genial day the foul may rife,
  Born to fome higher life, and hail fome brighter fkies.

THIS is the ftate of man ; to-day he puts forth
The tender leaves of hope, to-morrow bloffoms,
And bears his blufhing honours thick upon him ;
The third day comes a froft, a killing froft,
And—nips his root.

SO fond of liberty is man, that to reftrain him from any
thing, however indifferent, is fufficient to make that thing an
object of defire.

NO man ever did a defigned injury to another, without
doing a greater to himfelf.

MAN's chief good is an upright mind, which no earthly
power can beftow, nor take from him.

TAKE no advantage of the ignorance, neceffity or pro-
digality of any man, for that gain can never be bleft.

UPON whatfoever foundation happinefs is built, when that
foundation fails, happinefs muft be deftroyed ; for which reafon, it is wifdom to choofe fuch a foundation for it, as is not
liable to deftructive accidents.

IF happinefs be founded upon riches, it lies at the mercy of
theft, deceit, oppreffion, war and tyranny ; if upon fine houfes,
and coftly furniture, one fpark of fire is able to confume it ; if
upon wife, children, friends, health or life, a thoufand difeaf-
es, and ten thoufand accidents, have power to deftroy it ; but,
if it be founded upon the infinite bounty and goodnefs of God,
and upon thofe virtues that entitle to his favour, its foundation
is unmoveable, and its duration eternal.   PHA-

PHARAOH's DAUGHTER.

FAST by the margin of her native flood,
    Whose fertile waters are well known to fame,
Fair as the bord'ring flow'rs the princess stood,
    And rich in bounty as the gen'rous stream.
When, lo ! a tender cry afflicts her ear,
    The tender cry declares an infant's grief ;
Soon she, who melted at each mortal's care,
    With tend'rest pity sought the babe's relief.
The babe, adorn'd in beauty's early bloom,
    But to the last distress expos'd, appears,
His infant softness pleads a milder doom,
    And speaks with all the eloquence of tears.
The kind Egyptian gaz'd upon his charms,
    And with compassion view'd the weeping child ;
She snatch'd the little Hebrew to her arms,
    And kiss'd the infant—the sweet infant smil'd.
Again she clasps him with a fond embrace,
    Yet more she pities the young stranger's woe ;
She wip'd the tears that hung upon his face,
    Her own the while in pious plenty flow.
Now, cruel father, thy harsh law I see,
    And feel that rigour which the Hebrews mourn ;
O ! that I could reverse the dire decree,
    Which dooms the babe a wretch as soon as born !
But that, alas ! exceeds my slender pow'r—
    And must this tender innocent be slain ?
Poor harmless babe ! born in a luckless hour,
    Yet sweet as ever sooth'd a mother's pain.
Must thou, poor undeserving infant, die ?
    No ! in my bosom ev'ry danger shun ;
A princess shall thy parents loss supply,
    And thou art worthy to be call'd her son.

SENECA himself allows, that in conferring benefits, the present should always be suited to the dignity of the receiver. Thus the rich receive large presents, and are thanked for ac-
cepting

cepting them. Men of middling stations are obliged to be content with prefents fomething lefs, while the poor beggar, who may be truly faid to want indeed, is thought to be well paid if a fingle farthing rewards his warmeft folicitations.

SELF-DENIAL is the moft exalted pleafure; and the conqueft of evil habits is the moft glorious triumph.

THE true way to advance another's virtue, is to follow it; and the beft means to cry down another's vice, is to decline it.

HOW ought every teftimony of God's goodnefs to excite our love, our gratitude and praife! The fmalleft temporal advantage is a blefling, to which we have no title; if we have food and raiment, they are more than we deferve.

WHY are we commanded to pray, "Give us this day our daily bread," if not to teach us, among other things, our daily dependence upon God as the difpenfer of all our temporal bleffings? Our various wants return with the morning; and to whom fhould we look, but to him who is able to fupply them? We need his direction through the perplexities and difficulties of every day; and without his blefling and fupport, we can effect nothing to any valuable purpofe. In the evening, we feek reft in vain, unlefs he give flumber to the eye-lids, and fleep to the eyes? And as there are wants common to every family, and what all its members conftantly experience, they ought certainly to unite in fupplicating the fame divine goodnefs, and alfo in returning thanks for the mercies of which they have all been joint partakers.

THE neglect of any fpiritual duty, arifes from a declenfion of religion in the foul. Were we to live more under the fenfible enjoyment of divine love, we fhould be more active, vigorous, and fteady in the performance of every divine precept or command. The ways of God would not then appear either burthenfome or grievous, but as they truly are "Ways of pleafantnefs, and paths of peace."

THE difcontents of the poor are much eafier allayed, than thofe of the rich.   ON

ON GOD.

WHAT tho' no object strike upon the sight,
Thy sacred presence is an inward light.
What tho' no sound shall penetrate the ear,
To list'ning faith the voice of truth is clear.
Sincere devotion wants no outward shrine,
The centre of an humble soul is thine.
There may I worship, and there may'st thou raise
Thy seat of glory, and thy throne of grace;
Yea, fix (if Christ my advocate appear)
The strict tribunal of thy justice there.
Let each vain thought, and each impure desire,
Meet in thy wrath with a consuming fire.
Thou too canst raise (tho' punishing for sin)
The joys of peaceful penitence within;
Thy justice and thy mercy both are sweet;
Thou mak'st our sufferings and salvation meet.
Befal me then, whatever God shall please,
His wounds are healing and his griefs give ease;
He is the true physician of the soul,
Applies the med'cine that can make it whole.
I'll do, I'll suffer, whatsoe'er he wills;
I see his aim thro' all these transient ills:
'Tis to ensure a salutary grief,
To fit the mind to absolute relief;
Till purg'd from ev'ry false and finite love,
Dead to the world, alive to things above;
The soul renew'd, as in its first form'd youth,
Shall worship God in spirit and in truth.

NONE should be so implacable, as to refuse an humble submission; he whose very best actions must be seen with favourable allowance, cannot be too mild, moderate and forgiving.

A PASSIONATE temper renders a man unfit for advice; deprives him of his reason; robs him of all that is great or noble in his nature; it makes him unfit for conversation;
destroys

deftroys friendfhip ; changes juftice into cruelty ; and turns all order into confufion.

THERE is no greater fign of a mean and fordid fpirit, fays Cicero, than to doat upon riches ; nor is any thing more magnificent, than to lay them out freely in acts of bounty and liberality.

A FIRM truft in the affiftance of an Almighty being, naturally produces patience, hope, cheerfulnefs, and all other difpofitions of mind, that alleviate thofe calamities which we are not able to remove.

DIVINE Providence always places the remedy near the evil. There is not any duty, to which Providence has not annexed a blefling ; nor any affliction, for which he has not provided a remedy.

A GOOD confcience, and a contented mind, will make a man happy in all conditions.

HE that overcomes his paffions, conquers his greateft enemies.

THE defire of being thought wife, is often an hinderance to being fo ; for fuch a one is more folicitous to let the world fee what knowledge he hath, than to learn that which he wants.

A WISE man endeavours to fhine in himfelf; a fool to outfhine others. The firft is humbled by the fenfe of his own infirmities ; the laft is lifted up by the difcovery of thofe which he obferves in others. The wife man confiders what he wants ; and the fool, what he abounds in. The wife man is happy when he gains his own approbation ; and the fool, when he recommends himfelf to the applaufe of thofe about him.

NO knowledge, which terminates in curiofity and fpeculation, is comparable to that which is of ufe ; and of all ufeful knowledge, that is moft fo which confifts in a due care and juft notion of ourfelves.

OF

OF all parts of wifdom, the practice is the beft. Socrates was efteemed the wifeft man of his time, becaufe he turned his acquired knowledge into morality, and aimed at goodnefs more than greatnefs.

THO' it be an argument of a great wit, to give ingenious reafons for many wonderful appearances in nature; yet, it is an evidence of fmall judgment, to be pofitive in any thing but the knowledge of our own ignorance.

THE higheft learning is, to be wife; and the greateft wifdom is, to be good.

INSTEAD of labouring in nice learning and intricate fciences; inftead of trifling away precious time upon the fecrets of nature, or myfteries of ftate, it were better to feek that only which is really and fubftantially good.

TRUE philofophy, fays Plato, confifts more in fidelity, conftancy, juftice, fincerity, and in the love of our duty, than in a great capacity.

THE beft people need afflictions for trial of their virtue. How can we exercife the grace of contentment, if all things fucceed well? Or that of forgivenefs, if we have no enemies?

THE moft excellent of all moral virtues, is to have a low efteem of ourfelves, which has this particular advantage, that it attracts not the envy of others.

IF a man fhould forfake a kingdom, and all the world, if he cannot renounce himfelf, he has hardly done any thing.

WHATSOEVER convenience may be thought to be in falfhood and diffimulation, it is foon over; but the inconvenience of it is perpetual, becaufe it brings a man under a continual jealoufy and fufpicion; fo that he is not believed when he fpeaks truth, nor trufted, when perhaps he means honeftly.

Reflection

Reflection by a Perſon in his Sixtieth Year.

PLAC'D on the world's diſtracted ſtage;
  And forc'd to act a joyleſs part,
Why ſhould I ſhrink at creeping age,
  Which warns me friendly to depart?
Why do I rather not rejoice,
  That I my hapleſs courſe have ran?
And rul'd by wiſdom's Heavenly voice,
  Make my laſt exit like a man.
Fierce, tho' affliction's billows roll,
  And deep diſtreſs deforms the ſcene;
If innocence ſecure the ſoul,
  Vain is their rage, the tumult vain.
Serene ſhe ſmiles, yet ſmiling ſighs,
  To quit this darkſome, dull abode,
Wiſhing to win her native ſkies,
  And find a laſting reſt in God.
Weari'd, then let me quit the ſtrife,
  Kind Heav'n aſſent and ſet me free!
For why ſhould I be fond of life,
  When life itſelf is tir'd of me!

ORDER is Heaven's firſt law, and this confeſt,
Some are, and muſt be, greater than the reſt;
More rich, more wiſe—but who infers from hence,
That ſuch are happier, ſhocks all common ſenſe.

BE careful not to endeavour to imitate other men's ways, except it be in their eſſential virtues.

THE diſtribution of all our temporal mercies is wiſely regulated by the hand of God. Some men are favoured with a large ſhare of worldly bleſſings; ſome with things juſt neceſſary and convenient; while ſome, equally deſerving, have ſcarcely whereon to lay their heads. The diſpoſal of thoſe things is the work of God: He maketh poor and maketh rich; he bringeth low and lifteth up, and none have a right to ſay to him, what doeſt thou?   I   EVERY

EVERY ferious perfon muſt trace the marks of
ble hand in all the variegated paths of life.   He mu
ledge, that it is noṭ in man who walketh, to direct
yea, he will rejoice to find they are ordered by the Loi
lighteth in his way. And were we more obſervant of
Providence, many of our enquiries would be ne
ſhould ſee the path marked out before us, and if a
through miſtake we ſhould turn either to the right
the left, we ſhould hear a ſtill ſmall voice whiſperi
" this is the way, walk in it."

The contented Swain.

I SEEK not India's pearly ſhore,
Nor weſtern climes will I explore ;
Nor midſt the world's tumultuous ſtrife,
Will waſte what now remains of life.
I ſeek not aught that me may lead,
From tufted grove or flow'ry mead ;
Or from my native ſwains among,
Who liſten to my artleſs ſong.
For nought Golconda's gems avail,
In this ſequeſter'd humble dale ;
Nor joys can crowded cities yield,
Like thoſe of hill or daiſi'd field.
Calm as the ſummer ev'ning's ſun,
May here my glaſs of life be run !
And bright as is his parting ray,
My proſpect of a future day !
Mean while, the lab'ring hind to chear,
To wipe the widow's falling tear,
Such tranquil pleaſures will beſtow,
As riot's ſons can never know.
This, this be mine ! the ſpeaking eye
Shall then the ſculptur'd ſtone ſupply ;
As o'er my turf the ruſtics bend,
The poor ſhall ſay, " here lies our friend."

LET your promifes be fincere, and fo prudently confidered, as not to exceed the reach of your ability ; he who promifes more than he is able to perform, difgraces himfelf ; and he who does not perform what he has promifed, is falfe to his friend.

THE immortal mind, perhaps, will quit a cottage with lefs regret than it would leave the fplendour of a palace ; and the breathlefs duft fleep as quietly beneath the graffy turf, as under the parade of a coftly monument. Thefe are infignificant circumftances, to a fpirit doomed to an endlefs duration of mifery or blifs.

AS the belief of a God is the foundation of all religion, there can be no religion without faith ; but as true religion includes virtue, religion can not be perfect without works.

AMAZ.'D, the wonders of thy God behold !
And meditate his mercies manifold.
Oh ! happy time, when fhaking off this clay,
The human foul at liberty fhall ftray
'Thro' all the works of nature ! fhall defcry
Thofe objects which evade the mortal eye ;
No diftance, then, fhall ftretch beyond its flight,
No fmallnefs 'fcape its penetrating fight ;
But, in their real effence, fhall be fhewn
Worlds unexplor'd, creations yet unknown.

REFLECTIONS.

WHAT, oh ! my heart, overflowing with happinefs ! are the fentiments that ought to fpring up in thee, when admitted, either in the folemnities of public worfhip, or the retirednefs of private devotion, into the more immediate prefence of thy Maker—who does not govern, but to blefs ! whofe divine commands are fent to fuccour human reafon in fearch of happinefs !

pinefs! Let thy law, Almighty! be the rule, and thy glory
the conftant end, of all I do. Let me not build virtue on any
notions of honour, but of honour to thy name. Let me not
fink piety in tne boaft of benevolence; my love of God in the
love of my fellow-creatures. Can good be of human growth!
No—it is thy gift, Almighty, and All-good! Let not thy
bounties remove the donor from my thought; nor the love of
pleafures make me forfake the fountain from which they flow.
When joys entice, let me afk their title to my heart: When
evils threaten, let me fee thy mercy fhining through the
cloud, and difcern the great hazard of having all to my wifh.
In an age of fuch licentioufnefs, let me not take comfort
from the number of thofe who do amifs; an omen rather
of public ruin, than of private fafety. Let the joys of the
multitude lefs allure than alarm me; and their danger, not
example, determine my choice. In this day of domineering
pleafures, fo lower my tafte as to make me relifh the comforts
of life. And in this day of diffipation, O give me thought
fufficient to preferve me from being fo defperate, as in this perpetual flux of things, and as perpetual fwarm of accidents, to
depend on to-morrow; a dependence that is the ruin of to-
day, as that is of eternity. Let my whole exiftence be ever
before me, nor let the terrors of the grave turn back my furvey. When temptations arife, and virtue ftaggers, let imagination found the final trumpet, and judgment lay hold on eternal life. In what is well begun, grant me to perfevere,
and to know, that none are wife, but they who determine
to be wifer ftill. And fince, O Lord! the fear of thee
is the beginning of wifdom, and, in its progrefs, its fecret
fhield, turn the world entirely out of my heart, and place
that guardian angel, thy bleffed fear, in its ftead. Turn out
a foolifh world, which gives its money for what is not bread;
which hews out broken cifterns, that hold no water; a world,
in which even they, whofe hands are mighty, have found nothing. There is nothing, Lord God Almighty! in Heaven,
in earth, but thee—I will feek thy face; blefs thy name; fing
thy praifes; love thy law; do thy will; enjoy thy peace;
hope thy glory, till my final hour! Thus fhall I grafp all that
can be grafped by man. This will heighten good, and foften
evil, in the prefent life; and when death fummons, I fhall
sleep

leep fweetly in the duft, till his mighty conqueror bids the
trumpet found, and then fhall I, through his merits, awake to
ternal glory.

* * * * * * *

ALL pleafures are imperfect here below;
Our fweeteft joys are mix'd with bitter woe;
The draught of blifs, when in our goblet caft,
Is dafh'd with grief, or fpilt before we tafte.

CONTENTED poverty's no difmal thing,
Free from the cares unwieldy riches bring;
At diftance, both alike deceive our view;
Nearer approach'd, they take another hue.
The poor man's labour relifhes his meat;
His morfel's pleafant, and his reft is fweet:
Not fo the rich, who find their weari'd tafte
Pall'd with the profpect of the cumb'rous feaft;
For what they have more than they can enjoy,
Inftead of fatisfying, does but cloy.

The Divine Prefence.

THE high and mighty King of Kings,
Whofe praife the whole creation fings,
Hath fix'd, in love to human kind,
His bleffed image in our mind.—
The lines are ftrong, the picture fair,
No need of anxious fearch and care;
Look but within, and ftrait appears,
The fignature all nature wears!
Where'er I am, howe'er oppreft,
This Heav'nly portrait in my breaft
Infpires, with confidence divine,
And comfort flows from ev'ry line!
Thro' dangers numberlefs I go,
Yet weather all the ftorms that blow—
To lead me to the peaceful fhore,
My God and guide is ftill before!

I 2

At

At night, before I close my eyes,
And in the morning, when I rise,
I pray for safety, health and grace,
And still the Lord before me place !
He sheds his odours round my head,
And makes me sleep secure in bed ;.
In all the labours of the day
He goes before and points the way !

    Soon as my passions wild prevail,
And faith and reason both assail ;
When strong temptations spread their net,
Before me still the Lord I set ;
His presence can the passions lay,
And teach them reason to obey ;
Temptation's charms soon disappear,
And truth succeeds when God is near !

    When sorrows upon sorrows roll,
And sharpest arrows pierce my soul ;
When deepest sunk in black despair,
I lift my eyes and heart in pray'r !
Just when all human help had fail'd,
And friend and neighbour nought avail'd,
This best of friends, in constant view,
Shews what himself alone can do !

    Thro' all the future ills of life,
Amidst contempt, reproach and strife,
I'll set the Lord before me still;
And live obedient to his will !
So when thro' death's dark vale I move,
He will a light before me prove ;
Conduct me safe to endless joy,
And mark me out some blest employ.

----◇⚬⚭⚭⚭⚭⚬◇----

WHEN the oil of grace actuates the soul, the wheels of
obedience move with celerity ; but when this is wanting, every
duty, if not neglected, will be indifferently performed.

                                                          TRUE

TRUE happiness is of a retired nature, and an enemy to pomp and noise; it arises, in the first place, from the enjoyment of one's self; and, in the next, from the friendship and conversation of a few select companions. It loves shade and solitude, and naturally haunts groves and fountains, fields and meadows: In short, it feels every thing it wants within itself, and receives no addition from multitudes of witnesses and spectators. On the contrary, false happiness loves to be in a crowd, and to draw the eyes of the world upon her. She does not receive any satisfaction from the applauses which she gives herself, but from the admiration which she raises in others. She flourishes in courts and palaces, theatres and assemblies; and has no existence, but when she is looked upon.

IF good we plant not, vice will fill the mind,
And weeds despoil the space for flow'rs design'd.
The human heart ne'er knows a state of rest,
Bad tends to worse, and better leads to best;
We either gain or lose, we sink or rise,
Nor rests our struggling nature 'till she dies;
Those very passions that our peace invade,
If rightly pointed, blessings may be made;
Then rise, my friend, above terrestrial aims,
Direct the ardour which your breast inflames
To that pure region of eternal joys,
Where fear disturbs not, nor possession cloys;
Beyond what fancy forms of rosy bow'rs
Or blooming chaplets of unfading flow'rs;
Fairer than e'er imagination drew,
Or poets warmest visions ever knew;
Press eager onward to those blissful plains,
Where one unbounded spring forever reigns.

LEARN to pursue virtue from the man that is blind, who never makes a step, without first examining the ground with his staff.

SET

SET bounds to your zeal by difcretion; to error by truth; to paffion by reafon; and to divifion by charity.

THE path of virtue is the path of peace; in that only we can travel with fafety, or rationally hope to enjoy permanent pleafures.

LET ufelefs riches ne'er engrofs my care,
The bane of piety, the mifer's pray'r;
Yet let my purfe the mod'rate ftore contain,
To fatisfy my wants, and eafe my pain;
And when the needy at my threfhold ftand,
To foothe their cares, and fill the craving hand.

CONTENT.

HAPPY the man (but oh! how few we find)
Who feels the pleafures of a tranquil mind!
Who meets all bleffings in content alone,
Nor knows a ftation happier than his own
No anxious cares difturb his peaceful breaft,
With life content, and with contentment bleft;
No pangs he feels to break his calm repofe;
No envy fears, for he no envy knows.
To man ftill faithful, and to God refign'd,
His body fubject to its lord, the mind.
He muft be good—for furely Heav'n ne'er meant,
Without ftrict virtue, to beftow content.
'Tis not the glory falfe ambition brings,
The wealth of mifers, or the pow'r of kings;
Nor all the fleeting joys by man poffefs'd,
Can give this earthly frame that Heav'nly gueft;
Whate'er the mufe of love or glory fings,
Virtue alone the facred ftranger brings.

CONSCIENCE diftafteful truths may tell,
But mark her facred leffons well!
Whoever lives with her at ftrife,
Lofes his better friend for life.

THE

THE line of human underftanding, is undoubtedly too fhort to fathom the depths of the divine difpenfations ; and the moft enlarged capacity too narrow, to comprehend the ways of infinite wifdom.

IT is defirable, for the inward peace and eafe of men's own minds within themfelves, that they fhould not be under the power of fretful paffions, and the lafting refentments of a revengeful fpirit ; but that they be meek and gentle, peaceable, and eafy to be reconciled ; which fweetnefs of difpofition, improved upon religious principles into a habit of meeknefs, is a virtue, reflecting upon itfelf that calm and fedate fatisfaction, which is in a peculiar manner a reward to itfelf ; nor is it lefs beneficial to the public, as being the great prefervative againft that beginning of ftrife, which Solomon elegantly compares to the letting out of water ; that is, the opening of a breach, which no man can be fure to ftop, before it proceeds to the moft calamitous events.

THERE is no material good that can yield that fubftantial happinefs, which is fuited to the nature and defires of the human mind ; and he who thinks to find it in any thing beneath the fun, is purfuing a phantom, that will elude his chafe ; and if it feem to loiter for his approach, it will only be to convince him of his folly, to fhew him a miftake that he never faw, and of which thoufands never thought, till their race terminated in that country, from whence none ever yet returned to own their error, or confefs their fhame.

WOULD you the bloom of youth fhould laft,
'Tis virtue that muft bind it faft ;
An eafy carriage wholly free
From four referve or levity ;
Good-natur'd mirth, an open heart,
And looks unfkill'd in any art ;
Thefe are the charms that ne'er decay,
Tho' youth and beauty fade away ;
And time, which all things elfe removes,
Still heightens virtue and improves.

BOAST

BOAST not of health or beauty, or the days of youth.
Delay not the care of the foul, in hopes that you will live to
old age, or that you can do all that is required of youth,
with refpect to religion, on a bed of affliction. Strive, by
the grace of God, ever to be in readinefs to go hence and
be with our Saviour, which is infinitely better than all that
this world can afford ; and then you may meet the king of
terrors with a placid countenance, and a heart that rejoiceth
in hope.

THEY enjoy life beft, who are beft prepared for death ;
who look not for more happinefs from this world, than it is
capable of giving ; who live righteoufly, foberly and pioufly ;
who pray to God for the bleffings they need, and receive
thankfully all good things as his gifts—and who can rejoice
in the animating hope of falvation, thro' a Redeemer.

WHEN you a wilder'd trav'ler meet,
Guide to the road his erring feet ;
Or to your roof, if late, invite,
And fhield him from the damps of night.
To ftill the voice of anguifh, try
To wipe the tear from forrow's eye ;
And every good you can, impart
With ready hand, and glowing heart,
So fhall ye pafs, from manhood's ftage,
Smoothly along the flope of age ;
Then from the pleafing journey reft,
In peaceful fleep, belov'd and bleft.

CONTENTMENT.

FORGET not that thy ftation on earth is appointed by
the wifdom of the eternal ; who knoweth thy heart, who feeth
the vanity of all thy wifhes, and who in mercy often denieth
thy requefts ; yet for all reafonable defires, for all honeft endeavours,

deavours, his benevolence hath appointed, in the nature of things, a probability of fuccefs. The uneafinefs thou feeleft, the misfortunes thou bewaileft, behold the root from whence they fpring, even thine own folly, thine own pride, thine own diftempered fancy ; murmur not therefore at the difpenfations of God, but correct thine own heart ; neither fay within thy-felf, if I had wealth or power, or leifure, I fhould be happy ; for know, they all of them bring to their feveral poffeffors their peculiar inconveniencies.

THE poor man feeth not the vexations and anxieties of the rich ; he feeleth not the difficulties and perplexities of power, neither the wearifomenefs of leifure, and therefore it is that he repineth at his own lot. But envy not the appearance of hap-pinefs in any man, for thou knoweft not his griefs. To be fatisfied with a little, is the greateft wifdom ; and he that en-creafeth his riches, encreafeth his cares ; but a contented mind is a hidden treafure, and trouble findeth it not. Yet if thou fuffereft not the allurements of fortune to rob thee of juftice or temperance, or charity or modefty, even riches themfelves fhall not make thee unhappy ; but hence fhalt thou learn, that the cup of felicity, pure and unmixed, is by no means a draught for mortal man.

Virtue is the race which God hath appointed him to run, and happinefs the goal which none can arrive at, till he hath finifhed his courfe, and received his crown in the manfions of eternity.

···❖····❖··◁◆◁◆◁◆◁◆◁◆◁◆◆···❖···❖···

An Hymn to Contentment.

LOVELY, lafting peace of mind,
Sweet delight of human kind,
Heav'nly born and bred on high
To crown the fav'rites of the fky,
With more of happinefs below
Than victors in a triumph know.
Whither, oh ! whither, art thou fled,
To lay thy meek contented head ?

What

What happy region doft thou pleafe
To make the feat of charms and eafe ?
   Ambition fearches all its fphere
Of pomp and ftate to meet thee there ;
Encreafing avarice would find
Thy prefence in its gold enfhrin'd ;
The bold advent'rer ploughs his way
'Thro' rocks, amidft the foaming fea,
To gain thy love, and then perceives
Thou wert not in the rocks and waves.
   The filent heart which grief affails,
Treads foft and lonefome o'er the vales ;
Sees daifies open, rivers run,
And feeks, as I have vainly done,
Amufing thought ; but learns to know
That folitude's the nurfe of woe.
No real happinefs is found
In trailing purple on the ground ;
Or in a foul, exalted high,
To range the circuit of the fky ;
Converfe with ftars above, and know
All nature in its forms below ;
The reft it feeks—in feeking dies,
And doubts at laft for knowledge rife.
'Twas thus, as under fhade I ftood,
I fung my wifhes to the wood ;
And, loft in thought, no more perceiv'd
The branches whifper'd as they wav'd ;
It feem'd as all the quiet place
Confefs'd the prefence of the grace,
When thus fhe fpoke—go rule thy will,
Bid thy wild paffions all be ftill ;
Know God, and bring thy heart to know
The joys which from religion flow.
Then ev'ry grace fhall prove its gueft,
And I'll be there to crown the reft.
Oh ! by yonder mofy feat,
In my hours of fweet retreat,
Might I thus my foul employ,
With fenfe of gratitude and joy.

Rais'd

Rais'd, as antient prophets were,
In Heav'nly vifion, praife, and pray'r ;
Pleafing all men, hurting none,
Pleas'd and blefs'd with God alone.
Then while the gardens take my fight,
With all the colours of delight,
While filver waters glide along,
To pleafe my ear and court my fong,
I'll lift my voice, and tune my ftring,
And thee, great Source of Nature, fing !
The fun, that walks his airy way,
To light the world and give the day ;
The moon, that fhines with borrow'd light,
The ftars, that glad the gloomy night,
The feas, that roll unnumber'd waves,
The wood, that fpreads its fhady leaves,
The field, whofe ears conceal the grain,
The yellow treafure of the plain ;
All of thefe, and all I fee
Shou'd be fung, and fung by me ;
They fpeak their Maker as they can,
But want, and afk, the tongue of man.
Go fearch among your idle dreams,
Your bufy or your vain extremes,
And find a life of equal blifs,
Or own the next begun in this.

GRATITUDE.

THERE is not a more pleafing exercife of the mind,
than gratitude. · It is accompanied with fuch an inward fatif-
faction, that the duty is fufficiently rewarded by the performance. It is not like the practice of many other virtues, difficult and painful, but attended with fo much pleafure, that
were there no pofitive command which enjoined it, nor any recompence laid up for it hereafter, a generous mind would indulge in it for the natural gratification that accompanies it. If
gratitude is due from man to man, how much more from man

K   .to

to his Maker. The Supreme Being does not only confer upon us thofe bounties, which proceed more immediately from his hand, but even thofe benefits which are conveyed to us by others. Every blefiing we enjoy, by what means foever it may be derived upon us, is the gift of him who is the great Author of Good, and Father of Mercies.

WHEN thou haft done a kindnefs, or good office to any, be fure thou boaft not of it. It is the employment of a great foul, rather to do things worthy to be admired, than to admire what himfelf hath done.

NOTHING but virtue is capable of making us happy; if other advantages contribute thereto in fome meafure, it is only in as much as virtue bears them company.

SUPINENESS and effeminacy have ruined more conftitutions, than were ever deftroyed by exceffive labours; moderate exercife, far from prejudicing, ftrengthens and confolidates the body.

WE ought never to think too lightly of other people's complaints; but to regard the forrows of our fellow-creatures with fentiments of humanity and compaffion.

MAN fhould weigh well the nature of himfelf,
The varying frailnefs of this flattering world,
And the true excellence of Heav'n's high Lord;
Then would he this defpife, and truft in him.
The world deceives us all. In God is truth.
Let not thy riches or thy power prevail
To fwell thy bofom with conceits of pride;
Look back, remember thofe thou haft feen high,
And mark, if thou haft never feen them fink;
Let this teach thee. One end awaits us all!
And when inevitable death commands,
That we fhould follow to his dreary realm,
Matters it much, if from a royal couch,
Or from a mattrefs, thrown upon the ground,
We rife to take our journey.

The

The Husbandman's Meditation in the Field.

WITH toilsome steps when I pursue,
 O'er breaking clods, the plough-share's way,
Lord! teach my mortal eye to view
 My native-dissoluble clay.
And when with seed I strew the earth,
 To thee all praises let me give,
Whose hand prepar'd me for the birth,
 Whose breath inform'd and bade me live.
Pleas'd, I behold the stately stem
 Support its bearded honour's load;
Thus, Lord! sustain'd by thee, I came
 To manhood, thro' youth's dang'rous road.
Purging from noxious herbs the grain,
 Oh! may I learn to purge my mind
From sin, rank weed of deepest stain,
 Nor leave one baleful root behind.
When blasts destroy the op'ning ear,
 Life, thus replete with various woe,
Warns me to shun, with studious care,
 Pride, my most deadly latent foe.
When harvest comes, the yellow crop
 Prone to the reaper's sickle yields;
And I beneath death's scythe must drop,
 And soon or late forsake these fields.
When future crops, in silent hoards,
 Sleep, for a while to service dead;
Thy emblem this, oh grave! affords,
 The path of life which all must tread.

EVENING HYMN.

INDULGENT God, whose bounteous care
 O'er all thy works is shewn,
Oh! let my grateful praise and pray'r
 Ascend before thy throne.
What mercies has this day bestow'd,
 How largely hast thou blest,
My cup with plenty overflow'd,

And

And with content my breaſt.
Safe, 'midſt a thouſand latent ſnares,
    Thy careful hand has led,
And now, exempt from anxious cares
    I preſs the downy bed.
I fall this night into thy arms,
    Which I have prov'd ſo kind;
Oh! keep my body from all harms,
    And from all ſins my mind.
Let balmy ſlumbers cloſe my eyes,
    From pain and ſickneſs free;
And let my waking fancy riſe,
    To meditate on thee.
So bleſs each future day and night
    'Till life's fond ſcene is o'er,
And then, to realms of endleſs light,
    Oh! aid my ſoul to ſoar.

A little Ode to a little Maid, on her firſt going out after her Birth.

LITTLE zephyrs, loves and graces,
    Bid each chilling wind be laid,
Shelter'd in your warm embraces,
    See where comes my little maid.
With your guardian wings protect her,
    Every motion hover o'er;
Thro' her little path direct her,
    She ne'er ventur'd out before.
Forth ſhe comes, a new born creature,
    How her little blue eyes range!
Wonder ſits on every feature,
    All around is gay and ſtrange.
Couldſt thou, little maid; but paint me,
    What thy little fancy warms,
Or thy little tongue acquaint me
    Midſt this glitter what moſt charms.
To a ſtranger all's inviting,
    All a morning beauty wears;
Be the world, as now, delighting,

Tafte its joys, but not its cares!
Pity, gentleft child of Heav'n,
 Little maid will thee attend ;
Innocence is alfo given
 As thy guardian, as thy friend.
She fhall wake thy heart to pleafures,
 Such as virtue can difclofe ;
Give thee love and friendfhip's treafures,
 Strew thy path with many a rofe.
As in years, in wifdom growing,
 Never from her fide depart ;
Thro' thy future life ftill fhewing
 She had form'd thy youthful heart.
Let the falfe world ne'er confound thee,
 From its vices turn thine ear ;
Shun the bad examples round thee,
 Give them but a figh !—a tear !
Thus felf-guarded, thus defended,
 Thy experience fhall confefs,
Spite of what's by fools pretended,
 Virtue is true happinefs !
Such a blamelefs tract purfuing,
 Thy perfection's fenfe fhall tell ;
Oft this little ode reviewing,
 Little maid, I wifh thee well.

••◇••◇••❮❮❮❯❯❯❮❮❮❯❯❯••◇••◇••

THE CHURCH-YARD.

THINK, oh my foul, that while friends or ftrangers are
engaged on this fpot, and reading the fate of my departure
hence, thou wilt be fixed under a decifive and unchangeable
fentence, rejoicing in the rewards of time well improved, or
fuffering the forrows which fhall attend the abufe of it, in an
unknown world of happinefs or mifery.

MODESTY feldom refides in a breaft, that is not en-
riched with nobler virtues.

K 2   MODESTY

MODESTY is always, and juftly, fuppofed to be a con-comitant of merit; and every appearance of it is winning and prepoffeffing.

PRAISE beftow'd on living merit, is often found to in-jure the goodnefs it applauds.

THE ingratitude of the world, can never deprive us of the confcious happinefs of having acted with humanity ourfelves.

TO thee, oh God! thy fuppliant lifts his eyes,
 To thee Supreme, Omnipotent and Juft;
On thee alone for fuccour he relies,
 And in thy goodnefs places all his truft.
Teach me, with patience, meekly to fubmit
 To whatfoe'er thy wifdom judges beft;
To fay, with humble Job—the Lord thinks fit,
 " Giving or taking let his name be bleft."

SURE 'tis a ferious thing to die! My foul,
What a ftrange moment muft it be, when near
Thy journey's end, thou haft the gulph in view!
That awful gulph, no mortal e'er repafs'd,
To tell what's doing on the other fide.

THE wretch, condemn'd with life to part,
 Still, ftill on hope relies;
And ev'ry pang that rends the heart,
 Bids expectation rife.
Hope, like the glim'ring taper's light,
 Adorns and cheers the way;
And ftill, as darker grows the night,
 Emits a brighter ray.

MODESTY is not only an ornament, but alfo a guard to virtue. It is a kind of quick and delicate feeling in the foul.

foul, which makes her fhrink and withdraw herfelf from every thing that has danger in it. It is fuch an exquifite fenfibility, as warns her to fhun the firft appearance of every thing which is hurtful.

RICHES, in the hand of a beneficent man, are a bleffing to the public. Such an one is a fteward to Providence, and the noble means of correcting the inequalities of fortune, of relieving the miferable, and fpreading happinefs to all that are within the reach of his acquaintance.

The Wife's Confolation to her Hufband under Affliction.

NO more, lov'd partner of my foul,
  At difappointment grieve,
Can flowing tears our fate controul,
  Or fighs our woes relieve ?
Adverfity is virtue's fchool,
  To thofe who right difcern ;
Let us obferve each painful rule,
  And each hard leffon learn.
When wintry clouds obfcure the fky,
  And Heav'n and earth deform,
If fix'd the ftrong foundations lie,
  The caftle braves the ftorm.
Thus, fix'd on faith's unfailing rock,
  Let us endure awhile
Misfortune's rude impetuous fhock,
  And glory in our toil.
Ill fortune cannot always laft ;
  Or, tho' it fhould remain,
Yet we each painful moment hafte,
  A better world to gain—
Where calumny no more fhall wound,
  Nor faithlefs friends deftroy ;
Where innocence and truth are crown'd
  With never-fading joy.

GOOD

GOOD difcourfe is but the reflection or fhadow of wif-dom ; the pure and folid fubftance, is good actions.

THERE can be no true and fincere pleafure in any finful and, vicious courfe, tho' it be attended with all the pomp and fplendour of outward happinefs and profperity; for wherever fin and vice is, there muft be guilt ; and wherever guilt is, the mind will be reftlefs and unquiet.

INDUSTRIOUS wifdom often prevents what lazy folly thinks inevitable. Induftry argues an ingenious, great and generous difpofition of foul, by unweariedly purfuing things in the faireft light, and difdaining to enjoy the fruit of other men's labours, without deferving it.

GONCEITEDNESS and ignorance are a moft un-happy compofition ; for none are fo invincible as the half-witted, who know juft enough to excite their pride, but not fo much as to cure their ignorance.

ENDEAVOUR to be religious without fuperftition ; juft without rigour ; merciful without partiality ; cautious without fear ; valiant without rafhnefs ; and great without pride.

TO endeavour not to pleafe, is ill nature; altogether to ne-gleft it, folly ; and to overftrain for it, vanity and defign.

WHEN winds the mountain-oak affail,
  And lay its glories wafte,
Content may flumber in the vale
  Unconfcious of the blaft.

SWEET are the jefs'min's breathing flow'rs,
Sweet the foft falling vernal fhow'rs,
Sweet is the gloom the grove affords,
And fweet the notes of warb'ling birds ;
But not the groves, nor rains nor flow'rs,

Nor

Nor all the feather'd fongfters pow'rs,
Can ever fweet or pleafing be
O ! lovely freedom, without thee.

TEACH me between the two extremes to glide,
Not brave the ftream, nor fwim with ev'ry tide,
But more with charity, than zeal poffeft,
Keep my own faith, yet not condemn the reft.

RELIGION better qualifies all forts of men, and makes
them in public affairs the more ferviceable ; governors apter
to rule with confcience; and inferiors, for confcience fake, more
willing to obey.

LIBERALITY is never fo beautiful or engaging, as
when the hand is concealed which beftows the gift.

OECONOMY is no difgrace, it is better living on a
little, than outliving a great deal.

HOLY-DAYS.

SOME Chriftians to the Lord obferve a day,
    While others to the Lord obferve it not ;
And tho' thefe feem to choofe a diff'rent way,
    Yet both at laft to the fame point are brought.
Who for the obfervance pleads, may reafon thus—
    "As on this day our Saviour and our king
Perform'd fome glorious act of love for us,
    We keep the time in mem'ry of the thing."
Hence he to Jefus points his good intent,
    With pray'rs and praifes celebrates his name ;
And as to Chrift alone his love is meant,
    The Lord accepts it—and who dares to blame ?
For tho' the fhell indeed is not the meat,
    'Tis not rejected when the meat's within ;
Tho' fuperftition is a vain conceit,

Commemo-

Commemoration surely is no sin.
He likewise, that to days has no regard,
    The shadow only for the substance quits;
Towards his Saviour's presence presses hard,
    And that preferring outward things omits;
For thus within he seriously reflects,
    " My Lord alone I count my only good;
All empty forms for him my soul rejects,
    And only seek the riches of his blood.
All days, in Jesus, is my soul delight,
    The first and worthiest object of my care;
For whose dear sake all outward shews I slight,
    'Left aught but him should my devotion share."
Let not the observer therefore entertain,
    Against his brother any secret grudge;
And let the non-observer too refrain
    From censuring others whom he should not judge.
Thus both their motives bringing to the test,
    Our condescending Lord may both approve,
While each pursues the way he deems the best,
    For none can walk amiss who walk in love.

IF at any time you are pressed to do any thing hastily, be careful: Fraud and deceit are always in haste; but diffidence is the right eye of prudence.

IT is of little consequence to read eternal truths, if we pray not to obtain the gift of understanding them aright.

MEN take a great deal more pains for this world, than Heaven would cost them; and when they have it, do not live long to enjoy it.

THE time of life is the only time wherein we can prepare for another world; and oh! how short and uncertain is this time! How frail and uncertain is the life of man! What multitudes does death surprize in an hour, when they think nothing of it! How silently and insensibly does time slide
                                   away;

away; with what a winged fwiftnefs does it fly, and we cannot ftay its progrefs, ftop its courfe, or retard its hafty motion.

IN the morning fay to thyfelf, what fhall I do this day, which God has given me? How fhall I employ it to his glory? In the evening confider within thyfelf, and recollect, what have I done this day, and how have I fpent it?

TO prevent fpeaking evil of your neighbour, think no evil of him; and if you hear any, live in hopes that it is a miftake.

IF you defire to depend upon God, let it appear in every inftance of his Providence towards you: Be content with the want of thofe outward comforts which he thinks fit to deny you.

'TIS commonly obferved, that the firft ftep to wickednefs, is idlenefs; and indeed there is little hopes of any one being a good man, or a good Chriftian, who takes no care of his time.

OUR wants are daily, and the temptations which draw our hearts from God, to the things of this world, are alfo daily; and upon both thefe accounts, ought our prayers to be daily alfo.

LET it never enter into your head, that you are a man of merit. Be the only perfon, who neither knows or fpeaks of your own worth.

———————

THE well-taught philofophic mind,
    To all compaffion gives;
Cafts round the world an equal eye,
    And feels for each that lives.

IF friendlefs, in a vale of tears I ftray,
Where briers wound, and thorns perplex my way,
Lord let my fteady foul thy goodnefs fee,
And with ftrong confidence lay hold on thee;

                                                    With

With equal eye my various lot receive,
Refign'd to die, or refolute to live;
Prepar'd to kifs the fceptre or the rod,
While God is feen in all, and all in God.

———⊙—⊙—⊙—⊙—⊙—⊙———

WE muft never undervalue any perfon. The workman loves
not that his work fhould be defpifed in his prefence. Now
God is prefent every where, and every perfon is his work.

TO live contented, in a moderate eftate, we muft never confider thofe that have more, but thofe that have lefs than ourfelves.

———⊙—⊙—⊙—⊙—⊙—⊙———

THE BEECHEN SHADE.

TO this lone fhade, where peace delights to dwell,
    Oft let my unambitious mufe retire,
Here bid the vain tumultuous croud farewell,
    And praife my Maker with the wood-land choir.
How fhall I joy the dew-bright morn to view !
    With pleafure blufhing o'er the fair domain ;
The lowing herds and bleating flocks purfue,
    Thick ftrewed o'er the verdant flow'ry plain.
To fee fair nature, with pure delight,
    Give life and beauty to the rural fcene,
While tuneful birds, in ev'ry vocal grove,
    In fweet affemblage all around are feen.
To walk, by turns, the grove, the plain, the glade ;
    To trace the riv'let in its winding way,
At eve's approach, to hail my beechen fhade,
    And eye, with filent joy, the dancing fpray.
While thro' my veins a pleafing rev'rence thrills,
    How fhould I joy to fee the parting day,
Glide from the plains, the forefts and the hills,
    While Philomel begins her ev'ning lay.
Then with bold wings ftill upwards might I foar,
    And range, at will, the planetary field ;

The

The hand that guides the glowing worlds adore,
  And praife, in filent admiration, yield.
Hail, blifsful filence ! ftill this fhade attend,
  Be thou my conftant, never-failing gueft ;
Be thou my guide, my counfellor, my friend,
  Unrivall'd regent of my glowing breaft.
Let not the vain parade of wealth, or fhew,
  One wifh of envy in my breaft excite ;
Ah ! teach my heart this right'ous truth to know,
  That all the works of Providence are right.

SERENITY and gladnefs of heart, will attend a devout mind, when it maintains an intercourfe with the great Author of its Being. When we are in company with our God, with our Redeemer, with our deareft and beft of friends, our hearts will burn with love, or it with gratitude, fwell with hope, and triumph in the confcioufnefs of that prefence, which every where furrounds us ; or elfe we pour out our fears, our troubles, or our dangers to the great Supporter of our exiftence.

THE happinefs of a life religioufly fpent, plainly appears, from the poor and trifling enjoyments, that all thofe are forced to take up with, who live according to their own humour.

RELIGION is the refuge, in feafons of deepeft diftrefs ; it fmooths the chagrin of life, makes us eafy in all circumftances, and fills our fouls with the greateft peace that our natures are capable of. The contemplation of the life and fufferings of our Divine Leader, muft adminifter comfort in the fevereft affliction ; while the fenfe of his power and omnipotence, gives us humiliation in profperity.

ON RETIREMENT.

WHILE here fequefter'd from the bufy throng,
Let calm reflection animate my fong ;

L

May

May sweet retirement, with its soothing pow'rs
Compose each thought, and gild the passing hours;
And meek-ey'd peace, in whitest robes be seen,
To cheer the heart and make the mind serene;
Then while the world in busy scenes engage,
I'll shun the follies of a vicious age;
Freed from the dull impertinence of strife,
Serenely pass in solitude my life;
And when aurora ushers in the dawn,
And tuneful songsters hail the rising morn,
With grateful heart perform the ardent pray'r,
And thank kind Heav'n for its protecting care.
Then while the sun in radient splendour reigns,
And with its lustre decks the hills and plains,
Oft let me wander o'er the dewy vale,
And breathe sweet fragrance from the passing gale;
Or, led by fancy, frequent let me rove,
To some thick forest or some shady grove,
Where peaceful silence reigns throughout the scene,
And painted daisies deck the lovely green;
While gentle zephyrs, with their silken wings,
Display their beauties o'er the chrystal springs,
Or on the margin of a purling stream,
(Indulge my mind on friendship's pleasing theme)
Whose gentle murmurs calm the troubled breast,
And soothe each sorrow when the mind's distress'd.
Then when the sun, obedient to command,
Shall take his flight, and visit foreign land;
May pale-ey'd Cynthia, empress of the night,
With mildest lustre, shed her solemn light;
While twinkling stars dispense a friendly ray,
And gently guide the trav'ler on his way:
At this lone hour when solemn silence reigns,
And mournful Philomel renews her strains,
May no sad thought my peaceful mind molest,
Each murmur stifled, and each sigh suppress'd,
Save when compassion at another's woe
Shall cause the tears of tenderness to flow;
Freely I'll bear a sympathetic part,
And share the sorrows of the drooping heart;

With

With fervent pray'rs implore kind Heav'n to blefs,
And fondly ftrive to make their forrows lefs.
    Thus may my time in rural fhades be fpent,
Far from the world, enrich'd with calm content,
'Till death's cold hand fhall clofe thefe languid eyes,
And hope conduct me to yon blifsful fkies.

    O G L O R I O U S day! O day of peace, arife,
And with thy fplendours glad my longing eyes.
O time! which oft fo quickly glid'ft away,
Methinks thou ling'reft and defer'ft the day;
Juft like an arrow from a bow half ftrung,
Thy flagging pinions flowly fkim along.
Oh! with new vigour, urge thy flying courfe,
And ftretch each tendon with redoubled force;
That peace may flow like ocean's fwelling tide,
" And feas but join the regions they divide."

IT is the peculiar excellence of a good name, that it is out
of the reach of death, and is not buried in the grave, but rather
grows up from it. Solomon hath joined this good name, which
is better than precious ointment, with the day of one's death,
which is better than the day of one's birth, as it completes the
character of thofe that finifh their courfe well, and are faithful
unto death; whereas a great name, like the names of the great
ones of the earth, is often withered and blemifhed by death.

    W H A T is the blooming tincture of a fkin,
To peace of mind, to harmony within?
What the bright fparkling of the fineft eye,
To the foft foothing of a calm reply?
Can comelinefs of form, or fhape, or air,
With comelinefs of words or deeds compare?
No—thofe at firft th' unwary heart may gain,
But thefe, thefe only, can that heart retain.

RELIGION

RELIGION naturally tends to all that is great, worthy, friendly, generous and noble ; and the true spirit of it, not only composes, but cheers the soul. Though it banishes all levity of behaviour, all vicious and dissolute mirth—yet in exchange, it fills the mind with a perpetual serenity, and uninterrupted pleasure. The contemplation of divine mercy and power, and the exercise of virtue, are in their own nature so far from excluding all gladness of heart, that they are the principal and constant sources of it.

TEACH me, what all believe, but few possess,
    That life's best science is ourselves to know ;
The first of human blessings is to bless,
    And happiest he who feels another's woe :
Thus cheaply wise, and innocently great,
    While time's smooth sand shall regularly pass,
Each destin'd atom's quiet course I'll wait,
    Nor vainly break, nor wish to stop the glass.
And when in death my peaceful ashes lie,
    If e'er some tongue congenial speaks my name,
Friendship shall never blush to breathe a sigh,
    And great ones envy such an honest fame.

HE that can say to himself, I do as much good, and am as virtuous, as my most earnest endeavours will allow me, whatever is his station in the world, is as to himself possessed of the highest honour. If ambition is not thus turned, it is no other than a continual succession of anxiety and vexation. But when it has this cast, it invigorates the mind ; and the consciousness of its own worth is a reward, which it is not in the power of envy, detraction, or reproach, to take from it. Thus the seat of solid honour is in a man's own bosom ; and no one can want support, who is in possession of an honest conscience, but he who would suffer the reproaches of it for other greatness.

THERE are some men, in whom a deficiency of sense or wit gives no pain ; there are some, in whom abundance of both gives no pleasure.   The

The following lines are taken from a defcription of Hawkftone, an elegant feat in Shropfhire. The author of that defcription tells us, they were compofed by the owner of the abovementioned feat, when he was contemplating the aftonifhing fcenes around him in his own park, where the verfes are to be feen in a natural cavern of a vaft rock, from the top of which you command a very diverfified and romantic profpect.

WHILST all thy glories, O my God!
   Thro' the creation fhine,
Whilft rocks and hills, and fertile vales,
   Proclaim the hand divine—
O! may I view, with humble heart,
   The wonders of thy pow'r,
Difplay'd alike in wilder fcenes,
   As in each blade and flow'r.
But whilft I tafte thy bleffings, Lord!
   And fip the ftreams below,
O may my foul be led to thee,
   From whom all bleffings flow.
And, if fuch footfteps of thy love,
   Thro' this loft world we trace,
How far tranfcendant are thy works
   Throughout the world of grace!
Juft as before yon noon-tide fun,
   The brighteft ftars are fmall;
So earthly comforts are but fnares,
   'Till grace has crown'd them all.

Epitaph on a Country Clergyman.

STILL, like his Saviour, known by breaking bread,
The rich he entertain'd, the needy fed—
Of humour eafy, and of life unblam'd,
The friend delighted, while the prieft reclaim'd:
The friend, the father, and the hufband gone,
The prieft ftill lives in th' recording ftone,
Where pious eyes may read his praifes o'er,
And learn each grace his pulpit taught before.

THE

THE bent and inclination of a virtuous man is towards silence, as much as possible, because the principal light and knowledge of this life, consists in being thoroughly acquainted with the depth and greatness of his own ignorance. So that those who make great progress in human sciences, for the most part become peremptory and decisive : On the contrary, the proficients in the science of God become more reserved, more inclind to silence, less addicted to their own sense, and less venturesome to judge of others, because they discover more and more how uncertain and obscure our knowledge is; how much we often deceive ourselves in the things we think we know best ; how many faults and errors we run into by haste and precipitation in judging ; and what disorders are often caused by rash judgments and advices.

Inscription for an Hermitage.

FOND man, retire to this lone cell,
And bid the busy world farewell ;
Ah ! quit the city's noisy scene,
For pleasures tranquil and serene ;
Seek in this calm, this sweet recess,
The rose-lip'd cherub—happiness ;
That haunts the hermit's mossy floor,
And simple peasant's rural door.
How pleasant is yon oak's brown shade—
The spreading beach, th' adjacent glade ;
The chrystal streams, that smoothly glide ;
The warbling thrush, at eventide.
Fond man, here sweetly thou may'st spend
Thy fleeting days, nor fear thy end ;
Stealing thro' life, as thro' the plain,
Yon rill flows silent to the main.
Here (when in russet vest the morn
Walks o'er the mountain or the lawn)
Thy early orisons begin,
And live secure from woe and sin ;
Here too, at ev'nings sober hour,

Adore

Adore the great Almighty pow'r;
The Sovereign Ruler of the skies,
Forever just, and good, and wise.

PATIENCE will wipe away the streaming tear,
And hope will paint the pallid cheek of fear;
Content will always happiness supply,
And virtue calls a blessing from on high.

WHEN any body's misbehaviour disturbs you, dismiss the image of the injury, and bethink yourself whether you have not been guilty of the same fault. Such reflection is the shortest and most certain way of becoming truly wise and truly pious.

NO trees bear fruit in autumn, unless they blossom in the spring. To the end that our age may be profitable, and laden with ripe fruit, let all endeavour, that our youth may be studious, and flowered with the blossoms of learning and observation.

WE may judge of men by their conversation towards God, but never by Gods dispensation towards them.

TO learn to accommodate our taste to that portion of happiness, which Providence has set before us, is of all the lessons of philosophy, surely the most necessary. High and exquisite gratifications are not consistent with the appointed measures of humanity; and perhaps if we would fully enjoy the relish of our being, we should rather consider the miseries we escape, than too nicely examine the intrinsic worth of the happiness we possess.

WHEN a man is in company with his betters, it is as much more advisable to hear, than to speak, as it is better to reap, than to sow.

HE is the richest man, who desires no superfluity, and wants for no necessary.   RESTLESS

RESTLESS mortals toil for nought,
Blifs in vain from earth is fought ;
Blifs, a native of the fky,
Never wanders—mortals try ;
There you cannot feek in vain,
For to feek her is to gain.

COME gentle age ! to me thou doft appear
No cruel object of regret or fear ;
Thy ftealing ftep I unreluctant fee,
Nor would avoid, or wifh to fly from thee.

OTHER's good turns to thee be fure to tell,
But nothing fay, when thou thyfelf doft well.

SOME have pleafed themfelves with the thought, " That
departed fpirits fupply the place of guardian angels to their
friends ; that they delight to follow them in their folitary
walks, and watch their nightly flumbers, and make impreffions
on their fleeping fancy, to warn them of approaching dangers."
'Tis not unlikely, that the tempefts of human paffions are fometimes compofed by the foft infpiring whifpers of thofe propitious
beings, while the feats of joy have opened their glories in vi-
fionary fcenes to their fleeping imagination.

YOU may enjoy what you have, if you do not wifh for
more. Like a clear ftream, which glides fmoothly on, but by
endeavouring to encreafe the waters, it becomes a torrent.

OF greatnefs, and its pompous train,
What notions falfe we entertain !
The glitt'ring drefs, the fplendid feaft,
Thofe feeking moft, who know them lea
Our time, anxiety, and coft,
In the vain acquifition's loft.
The man we envy oft as bleft,
In fecret pines with care opprefs'd.

MANY

MANY fcripture parables and fimilitudes are taken from
the common actions of this life, that when our hands are em-
ployed about them, our hearts may the more eafily pafs thro'
them to divine and heavenly things.

EVERY thing is beautiful in its feafon; and it is the
wifdom of the prudent, fo to order the duties of their general
callings as Chriftians, and thofe of their particular callings in
the world, as that they may not clafh or interfere.

IT is related of the pious Philip Henry, that if any afked
his charity, whofe reprefentation of their cafe he did not like,
or who he thought did amifs to take that courfe, he would firft
give them an alms, and then mildly reprove them; labouring
to convince them that they were out of the way of duty; that
they could not expect God fhould blefs them in it, and would
not chide, but reafon with them. He would fay, if he fhould
tell them of their faults, and not give them an alms, the reproof
would look only like an excufe to deny his charity, and would
be rejected accordingly.

TO be over folicitous after praife, to be greedy of it, and
eager in purfuing it, and to feem in fome meafure to beg it, inftead of being the character of a great foul, is the moft certain
fign of a vain and light difpofition, which feeds upon the wind,
and takes the fhadow for the fubftance.

THE ANTS.

SO when the ants, a fmall induftrious train,
Embodied rob fome golden heap of grain,
Studious, ere ftormy winter frowns, to lay
Safe in their darkfome cells the treafur'd prey:
In one long track the dufky legions lead
Their prize in triumph, thro' the verdant mead;
Here bending with the load, a panting throng,
With force conjoin'd, heave fome huge grain along;
Some lafh the ftragglers to the tafk affign'd,
Some to their ranks the bands that lag behind;

They

They croud the peopled path in thick array,
Glow at the work, and darken all the way.

H O W blefs'd the man, who, like thefe infects, wife,
   Exerts his powers to lay up Heav'nly food;
Convinc'd, that nought like this beneath the fkies
   Deferves his care, and ought to be purfu'd.

   WOULD you in fafety plough th' inconftant tide,
The helm let prudence ever watchful guide.
She fhuns the deep, where mountain-billows roar,
And fhuns alike the fhallows and the fhore.
   The few, by precept or experience wife,
Who know the mean, the golden mean, to prize,
With equal fcorn reject a fordid ftate,
And the gilt forrows of the vainly great.
Fix'd in that point, where all the virtues reft,
Between th' extremes with peaceful pleafure bleft,
They know to curb irregular defires,
When av'rice tempts them, or ambition fires.

POSTS of preferment, and the marks of refpect annexed
to them, may flatter the ambition and vanity of mankind, but
in themfelves include no real glory or folid greatnefs, as they
are foreign to them—as they are not always the proof and reward of merit—as they add nothing to the good qualities either
of body or mind—as they correct none of our faults, but often,
on the contrary, ferve only to multiply and make them more
remarkable, by making them confpicuous, and exhibiting them
in a ftronger light.

I T is virtue alone which fixes the price of every thing, and
is the fole fource of folid glory and real greatnefs.

W I T is commonly looked upon with a fufpicious eye, as
a two-edged fword, from which not even the facrednefs of
friendfhip can fecure. It is more efpecially dreaded in women.

A

A MAN may be referved and modeft in the midft of riches
and honours, as he may be proud and avaricious in the obfcurity of a poor and wretched life.

TIME, always precious, can never be more fo, than in
our early years; the firft ideas make the ftrongeft and moft lafting impreffion.

NUMBERLESS are the branches of good nature!—
Numberlefs are the benefits we ourfelves receive by it, and confer on others!

MERE good humour, if abufed, will degenerate into its
reverfe; but good nature is always the fame, and incapable of
changing; like the divine fource, of which it is an emanation,
it returns injuries with benefits; it endeavours to work on the
bad heart that offers them, by foft perfuafion, and pities what
it cannot mend.

WHAT tho' to-day opprefs'd with various woes?
To-morrow's dawn may happier fcenes difclofe.
The bounteous pow'r that o'er wide nature reigns,
Now bids ftern winter blaft the freezing plains;
And now recalls the fpring, the fpring returns,
Each face now fmiles, and ev'ry bofom burns;
New beauty burfts upon the ravifh'd fight,
And all around is joy, and life, and light.

THRO' life let manly fortitude prevail,
Whate'er the current and whate'er the gale;
Prefs forward ftill, and ev'ry adverfe tide
Let thy flow, perfevering bark, divide.
But when too ftrong the fav'ring breeze you find,
Furl the broad fail, nor truft the faithlefs wind.

To MIRA, with a Watch.

MIRA, this machine, you'll find,
Suits a moralizing mind.

Has

Has it motion ? 'Tis as clear
Action is man's proper fphere.
Equal fhould its progrefs prove,
So thro' life let Mira move.
When you forward urge its pace,
Think it may be Mira's cafe ;
In my paffage to the fky,
Have I linger'd ?—let me fly !
Backwards are the hands convey'd,
To the points from whence they ftray'd ?
Blufh not, Mira ! to untread
Steps that wifdom never led.
If it ftand, reflecting fay,
Time for no machine will ftay ;
Heav'n obferves, and, will it find
Mira with him, or behind ?
Mark its hands with thanks to Heav'n,
For each hour and minute giv'n ;
Giv'n as means to make us wife ;
Giv'n to form us for the fkies.
Falfe if either hand be view'd,
Some internal fault conclude,
Thus if Mira's life fhould fin,
Let her firft reform within.
When it ftrikes the hour, admit
Silence is not always fit.
Ev'ry day its tafk purfu'd,
Hints how thine muft be renew'd.
Say, when winding up, alas !
Human wheels, like thofe of brafs
Soon their functions would forego,
Nought if foreign hand beftow.
If all day it acted right,
When fhe hangs it by at night,
Then let Mira afk her heart,
How have I perform'd my part ?
If it err'd, let Mira pray,
Heav'n forgive my faults to-day !
For its ufe, my prefent prize,
All befides neglect—defpife.

Shine its trinkets as they will,
Trinkets are but trifles still.
Mira ! when at court array'd
All in jewels, and brocade,
If at heart no merit dwell,
If no deeds that merit tell,
Tho' a lord should smile, or king,
Thou'rt a glit'ring, useless thing.
If whate'er its present praise,
All its pow'r to serve decays,
Means to mend it vainly try'd,
When you cast it from your side ;
On a life of virtue past,
Joyful retrospection cast ;
But let Mira think again,
Only virtue past were vain ;
Perseverance, 'till we die,
Wins the Christian's crown on high.

A WOMAN of true sense, will be always ambitious—not of gaining admiration, but of deserving it.

THERE is no being long, and sincerely happy, without being good ; which, as common an observation as it has been, yet wants to be made anew, by most, even of those, whom the world thinks both wise and happy.

GOOD humour shuns not an opportunity of obliging ; but good nature is industrious, in seeking out as many as it can. Good humour frequently promises more than is in its power to perform ; but good nature does more than it gives you reason to expect.

THE want of thought creates many mischiefs among mankind ; and this is the reason that none ought to speak, 'till they have first reflected on every thing that may possibly be the consequence of what they speak.

M   IT

IT is indeed a dreadful thing, when people cannot refolve to content themfelves with the fphere in which they are placed by Heaven. It is this reſtlefnefs of the mind, that occaſions half the mifchiefs that befal mankind; and yet we are all, more or lefs, apt to have fome fhare of it. Every one wifhes for fomething he has not, and that hinders him from enjoy-ing, properly, what he is poffeffed of. We fancy we know better than him that made us, what would befit us, and accufe Providence of partiality, in the lot affigned to us.

LIFE is an uncertain ocean; numberlefs, namelefs dan-gers, lurk beneath the faireſt furface. No one, at his firſt em-barkation, can promife to himfelf that he fhall go through his voyage, unruffled with the ſtorms which from above, below, and every where, furround. Who then would not be glad to fecure fome friendly bark at hand, whofe kind affiſtance, in cafe of a wreck, might fave him.

THE feeds of thofe ſpiritual joys and raptures, which are to ſe up and nouriſh in the foul to all eternity, muſt be plant-ed in her, during her prefent ſtate of probation.

BEWARE thy meddling hand in ought to try,
That does beyond thy reach of knowledge lie,
But feek to know, and bend thy ferious thought,
To-fearch the profitable knowledge out;
So joys, on joys, forever will encreafe,
Wifdom fhall crown thy labours, and fhall blefs }
Thy life with pleafure, and thy end with peace. }

LET gratitude, in acts of goodnefs flow,
My love to God, in love to man below;
Be this my joy, to calm the troubled breaſt,
Support the weak, and fuccour the diſtreſt;
Direct the wand'rer, dry the widow's tear,
The orphan guard, the finking fpirits chear.
Tho' fmall my pow'r to act, tho' mean my ſkill,
God fees the heart, he judges by the will.

AN

AN EVENING THOUGHT.

NOW down the steep of Heav'n the source of day
Pursues, unwearied, his diurnal way ;
Mild shine his rays, his beams serene descend,
And o'er the earth a sweet effulgence send.
The blust'ring winds a pleasing silence keep,
And in their caves, with folded pinions, sleep.
No longer from the cloud descends the rain,
But a clear azure spreads th' etherial plain ;
A solemn, pleasing silence, hovers round,
And peace, with downy wing, o'erspreads the ground.
While silver Cynthia sheds her milder light,
And ushers in the awful reign of night.
  So when the lamp of life shall dimly burn,
And this frail frame to kindred dust return,
May the rude strife of earth-born passions cease,
And life's short journey terminate in peace.
May then no ▓▓▓▓▓▓▓▓▓▓▓▓▓ my
Or keen reflections discompose my breast
May then no fears, no dread of ills to come,
Make me shrink back with terror from the tomb ;
But when the awful mandate from on high
The sentence shall proclaim, that bids me die,
Resign'd and peaceful, let me bow my head,
And Heav'n enjoy, when number'd with the dead.

TO be too inquisitive, into things in which we have no concern, and which, with the utmost labour, assisted by the greatest learning, and strongest capacity, we can never be able to penetrate, is doubtless both a sin and a folly.

A MIND, eager to enquire into the minutest works of nature, will be insensibly led to a contemplation on the greatest ; and in all, we shall find sufficient for our astonishment, and the exciting in us such ideas of the great Author of Nature, as cannot fail to fill us with the highest sense of the infinity of his goodness to all his creatures ; and to us in particular, to

whom

whom alone, of all fublunary beings, he has given the power of reafon and reflection.

THERE is nothing requires a greater delicacy of fentiment and expreffion, than what we call raillery ; and a perfon muft be very polite indeed, who knows how to practife it, fo as not to give offence.

TO be merry ourfelves, or make fport for others, on the errors or miftakes of our friend or companion, is certainly very unkind ; but if our jeft is on the defects or infirmities of his perfon, it is really cruel.

The dying Chriftian to his Soul.

I.

VITAL fpark of Heav'nly flame !
Quit, oh quit ! this mortal frame—
Trembling, hoping, ling'ring, flying,
Oh ! the pain, the blifs of dying !
Ceafe, fond nature, ceafe thy ftrife,
And let me languifh into life.

II.

Hark they whifper, angels fay,
Sifter fpirit come away !
What is this abforbs me quite,
Steals my fenfes, fhuts my fight ;
Drowns my fpirits, draws my breath,
Tell me, my foul, can this be death ?

III.

The world recedes, it difappears !
Heav'n opens on my eyes—my ears
    With founds feraphic ring :
Lend, lend your wings ! I mount ! I fly !
Oh ! grave, where is thy victory ?
    Oh ! death where is thy fting ?

THO' plung'd in ills, and exercis'd in care,
Yet never let the noble mind despair :
For blessings always wait on virtuous deeds,
And tho' a late, a sure reward succeeds.

THE brightest hours of prosperity, have their clouds ; and
the stream of life, if it is not ruffled by obstructions, will grow
putrid by stagnation.

WHATEVER busies the mind, without corrupting it,
has at least this use, that it rescues the day from idleness; and
he that is never idle, will not often be vicious.

KNOWLEDGE is praised and desired by multitudes,
whom her charms could never rouse from the couch of sloth.

SINCE life itself is uncertain, nothing which has life for
its basis, can boast much stability.

OF him that hopes to be forgiven, it is indispensably required, that he forgive.

FEW are placed in a situation so gloomy and distressful, as
not to see every day beings yet more forlorn and miserable,
from whom they may learn to rejoice in their own lot.

A CONSTANT series of unattainable amusement, re-
laxes the tone of the mind, and renders it totally incapable of
application, study, or virtue.

TO insult over the miseries of an unhappy creature, is in-
human ; not to compassionate them, unchristian.

THE wickedness of a woman changeth her face, and dark-
eneth her countenance like sack-cloth.
As the climbing of a sandy way is to the feet of the aged,
so is a wife full of words to a quiet man.
A woman that will not comfort her husband in distress, maketh weak hands and feeble knees.   Eccles. xxv. chap.

M 2   Extract

Extract from Young's Resignation.

WHAT cannot resignation do?
    It wonders can perform;
That pow'rful charm, " thy will be done,"
    Can lay the loudest storm.
Our hearts are fasten'd to this world,
    By strong and tender ties;
And ev'ry sorrow cuts a string,
    And urges us to rise.
When Heav'n would kindly set us free,
    And earth's enchantments end,
It takes the most effectual means,
    And robs us of a friend.
Oh! how disorder'd our machine,
    When contradictions mix;
When nature strikes no less than twelve,
    And folly points at six.
They let unmark'd, and unemploy'd,
    Life's idle moments run
And, doing nothing for themselves,
    Imagine nothing done.
Dang'rous mistake—their fate goes on,
    Their dread account proceeds—
And their not doing, is set down,
    Amongst their darkest deeds.

IT was the practice of Vespasian, the Roman emperor, to call himself to an account every night, for the actions of the past day; and as often as he let slip one day without doing some good, he entered upon his diary this memorial—
" I have lost a day."

THE grace of a wife delighteth her husband, and her discretion will fatten his bones.

A silent and loving woman is a gift of the Lord, and there is nothing so much worth, as a mind well instructed.

As the sun when it ariseth in the high heaven—so is the beauty of a good wife in the ordering of her house. Eccl. xxvi.

TO

TO hint at a fault, does more mischief, than speaking out; for whatever is left for the imagination to finish, will not fail to be overdone.

MEEKNESS is imperfect, if it be not both active and passive; if it will not enable us to subdue our own passions and resentments, as well as qualify us to bear, patiently, the passions and resentments of others.

ALEXANDER (says Seneca) had two friends, Clitus and Lysimachus; the one he exposed to a lion, the other to himself; he who was turned loose to the beast, escaped, but Clitus was murdered, for he was turned loose to an angry man.

COUNT that day lost, whose low descending sun
Views from thy hand no worthy action done.

LOVE the great God, with all thy might,
And know, whatever is, is right.
To his disposal always yield,
Who clothes the lillies of the field,
And trust his ever-watchful care,
Which numbers every single hair.
Each day the sacred pages view,
For these give pleasures ever new.
The truths that there conspicuous shine,
Proclaim their author all divine.
See here thy great Redeemer's love,
Who left the radiant realms above,
To perfect all the gospel plan,
Then dy'd, to save degen'rate man.
To him prefer thy ardent pray'r,
For such things as expedient are;
And if thy breast a mansion be,
Fit to receive the Heav'nly three,
The comforter shall soon be sent,
To fill the mind with sweet content;
And tho' the world, as all confess,
Can neither satisfy or bless,
Hence may'st thou draw that liquid store,
Which he that drinks of, thirsts no more.

WITH

————WITH Heaven's ennobling gifts
Benignly bleſt, the blooming Lucia ſhines :
Pleaſing her ſpeech, by nature taught to flow,
Strong and perſuaſive ſenſe, ſincere and clear.
Her manners greatly plain ; a noble grace
Self-taught, beyond the reach of mimic art,
Adorns her : Her calm temper, winning, mild,
Nor pity ſofter ; truth itſelf the ſource :
Conſtant in doing well, ſhe neither ſeeks,
Nor ſhuns applauſe. No baſhful merit ſighs
Near her neglected : Sympathizing, ſhe
Wipes off the tear from ſorrow's clouded eye
With kindly hand, and bids her heart to ſmile.

—◦—◦—◇——◇——◇——◇—◦—◦—

MEEKNESS may be called the pioneer of all the other
virtues, which levels every obſtruction, and ſmooths every difficulty, that might impede their entrance, or retard their pro-
greſs.

I F it were only for mere human reaſons, it would turn to
a better accoune, to be patient ; nothing defeats the malice
of an enemy, like a ſpirit of forbearance ; the return of rage
for rage cannot be ſo equally provoking. True gentleneſs,
like an impenetrable armour, repels the moſt pointed ſhafts of
malice ; they cannot pierce into his invulnerable ſhield, but
either fall harmleſs to the ground, or return to wound the hand
that ſhot them.

A MEEK ſpirit will not look out of itſelf for happineſs,
becauſe it finds a conſtant banquet at home ; yet by a ſort of Divine Alchymy, it will convert all external events to its own
profit, and be able to deduce ſome good, even from the moſt
unpromiſing ; it will extract comfort and ſatisfaction from the
moſt barren circumſtances ; " it will ſuck honey out of the
rock, and oil out of the flinty rock."

HONOURS and dignities are tranſient, beauty and
riches frail and fleeting, to a proverb. Would not the truly
wiſe,

wife, therefore, wifh to have fome one poffeffion, which they might call their own in the fevereft exigencies ? But this wifh can only be accomplifhed, by acquiring, and maintaining, that calm and abfolute felf-poffeffion, which as the world had no hand in giving, fo it cannot, by the moft malicious exertion of its power, take away.

AN amiable and wife woman will, always have fomething better to value herfelf on than outward advantages, which, however captivating, are ftill but fubordinate parts of a truly excellent character.

HOW cruel is it to extinguifh, by neglect or unkindnefs, the precious fenfibility of an open temper, to chill the amiable glow of an ingenious foul, and to quench the bright flame of a noble and generous fpirit ! Thefe are of higher worth, than all the documents of learning ; of dearer price, than all the advantages which can be derived from the moft refined and artificial mode of education.

THE beft of men, and the beft of books, can do us good, only fo far as they turn us from themfelves, and every human comfort, to feek and receive every kind of good, from God alone.

TO defire to communicate good to every creature, in the degree we can, and it is capable of receiving from us, is a divine temper ; for thus God ftands unchangeably difpofed towards the whole creation.

·—◦—◆◆◆◆◆◆—◦·

IN vain thou hop'ft for blifs on this poor clod ;
Return, and feek thy Father and thy God.
Yet think not to regain thy native fky,
Borne on the wings of vain philofophy.
Myfterious paffage ! hid from mortal eyes ;
Soaring you'll fink, and finking you will rife.
Let humble thoughts thy wary footfteps guide ;
Regain by meeknefs, what thou loft by pride.

LET

LET thy flock clothe the naked, and thy table feed the
hungry ; deliver the poor from oppreſſion, and let thy converſation be above. Thus ſhalt thou " rejoice in hope," and look
forward to the end of life, as the conſummation of thy felicity.

WHAT an example is Job, to ſuch as have loſt their ſub-
ſtance all at once, by unforeſeen misfortunes :—" The Lord
gave—the Lord hath taken away. Bleſſed be the name of the
Lord."

HUMANITY.

AH me ! how little knows the human heart,
   The pleaſing taſk of ſoft'ning other's woe ;
Stranger to joys, that pity can impart,
   And tears ſweet ſympathy can teach to flow.
If e'er I've mourn'd my humble, lowly ſtate ;
   If e'er I've bow'd my knee at fortune's ſhrine;
If e'er a wiſh eſcap'd me, to be great,
   The fervent pray'r, humanity, was thine.
Pity the man, who hears the moving tale
   Unmov'd, to whom the heart-felt glow's unknown ;
On whom the widow's plaints could ne'er prevail,
   Nor made the injur'd wretch's cauſe his own.
How little knows he th' extatic joy,
   The thrilling bliſs of chearing wan deſpair ;
How little knows the pleaſing, warm employ,
   That calls the grateful tribute of a tear.
The ſplendid dome, the vaulted roof to rear,
   The glare of pride and pomp, be grandeur thine ;
To wipe from mis'ry's eye the wailing tear,
   And ſoothe th' oppreſſed orphan's woes, be mine.
Be mine the bluſh of modeſt worth to ſpare,
   To change to ſmiles affliction's riſing ſigh ;
The kindred warmth of charity to ſhare,
   Till joy ſhall ſparkle from the tear-fill'd eye.
Can the loud laugh, the mirth inſpiring bowl,
   The dance, or choral ſong, or jocund glee,
Affect the glowing, ſympathizing ſoul,
   Or warm the breaſt, humanity, like thee ?

A C-

ACCEPTABLE SACRIFICE.

H E that keepeth the law, bringeth offerings enough : He that taketh heed to the commandment, offereth a peace-offering : He that requiteth a good turn offereth fine flour : And he that giveth alms, facrificeth praife. To depart from wickednefs, is a thing pleafing to the Lord ; and to forfake unrighteoufnefs, is a propitiation. Thou fhalt not appear empty before the Lord ; for all thefe things are to be done, becaufe of the commandment. The offering of the righteous maketh the altar fat, and the fweet favour thereof is before the Moft High! The facrifice of a juft man is acceptable, and the memorial thereof fhall never be forgotten. Eccles. xxxv.

W E fee almoft every day, the unexpected death of our friends and our enemies; we fee new graves often opened for men older and younger than ourfelves ; for the cautious and the carelefs, the diffolute and the temperate ; for men, who like us, were providing to enjoy or improve hours now irreverfibly cut off; we fee all this, and yet, inftead of living, let year glide after year, in preparations to live.

A M A N that fafteth for his fins, and goeth again and doeth the fame, who will hear his prayer ? or what doth his humbling profit him. Eccles. xxxiv. 26.

T H E mind is never fo fenfibly difpofed to pity the fufferings of others, as when it is itfelf fubdued and foftened by calamity. Adverfity diffufes a kind of facred calm over the breaft, that is the parent of thoughtfulnefs and meditation.

H E that looks upon the bufinefs and buftle of the world, with the philofophy with which Socrates furveyed the fair at Athens, will turn away at laft with his exclamation, " how many things are here which I do not want."

W H I L E affliction prepares us for felicity, we may confole ourfelves under its preffures, by remembering, that they are no particular marks of divine difpleafure, fince all the diftreffes of perfecution have been fuffered by thofe, " of whom the world was not worthy;" and the Redeemer of man and himfelf was " a man of forrows, and acquainted with grief."

I F

IF thou haft gathered nothing in thy youth, how canft thou find any thing in thine age?

Much experience is the crown of old men, and the fear of God is their glory.

Oh, how great is he that findeth wifdom! Yet is there none above him that feareth the Lord! The fear of the Lord is the beginning of his love; and faith is the beginning of cleaving unto him.

OF all the virtues, there are none ought more to be inculcated, into the mind of a young girl, than modefty and meeknefs. Vanity and pride are perpetually endeavouring to force their way into the heart; and too much care cannot be taken to repulfe their efforts.

WE muft, in this world, gain a relifh of truth and virtue, if we would be able to tafte that knowledge and perfection, which are to make us happy in the next.

The Governess: A Simile.

AS when blithe lambs their vernal revels keep,
Bound from the turf, and o'er the hillocks leap;
Now harmlefs try to butt, then run away;
Now wearied feed, and thus confume the day—
Th' indulgent fhepherdefs attentive lies,
Left from the woods fome fudden foe fhould rife,
And as they play, her harmlefs flock furprize.
So, the fage governefs, whofe conftant care
By wifdom's dictates, forms the tender fair;
When her gay female throng, to fport inclin'd,
Sufpend the nobler pleafures of the mind,
With jealous eyes each motion does furvey,
Left they fhould fwerve from virtue in their play.

CHILDREN, like tender oziers, take the bow,
And as they firft are fafhion'd, always grow;
For what we learn in youth, to that alone
In age we are by fecond nature prone.

Extract

Extract from Young's Night Thoughts.

THE chamber, where the good man meets his fate,
Is privileg'd beyond the common walk
Of virtuous life, quite in the verge of Heav'n.
Fly, ye profane ! if not draw near with awe,
Receive the blessing, and adore the hand
That threw in this Bethseda your disease.
If unrestor'd by this, despair your cure ;
For here, resistless demonstration dwells—
A death-bed's a detector of the heart ;
Here tir'd dissimulation drops her mask,
Thro' life's grimace, that mistress of the scene !
Here real, and apparent, are the same.
You see the man, you see his hold on Heav'n,
If found his virtue, as Philander's found,
Heav'n waits not the last moment, owns her friends
On this side death, and points them out to men—
A lecture silent, but of sov'reign pow'r !
To vice, confusion—and to virtue, peace.

***

IT is a certain sign of an ill heart, to be inclined to defamation. They who are harmless and innocent, can have no gratification that way ; but it ever arises from a neglect of what is laudable in a man's self, and an impatience of seeing it in another.

TO forbear replying to an unjust reproach, and overlook it, with a generous, or (if possible) with an entire neglect of it, is one of the most heroic acts of a great mind.

EVERY appearance of amiable simplicity, or of honest shame, nature's hasty conscience, will be dear to sensible hearts ; they will carefully cherish every such indication in a young female ; for they will perceive, that it is this temper, wisely cultivated, which will one day make her enamoured of the loveliness of virtue and the beauty of holiness ; from which she will acquire a taste for the doctrines of religion, and a spirit to perform the duties of it.

N   THE

T H E hypocrify of affuming virtues, which are not inhe-
rent in the heart, prevents the growth and difclofure of thofe
real ones, which it is the great end of education to cultivate.

G O O D difpofitions, of themfelves, will go but a very
little way, unlefs they are confirmed into good principles. And
this cannot be effected, but by a careful courfe of religious inftruction, and a patient and laborious cultivation of the moral
temper.

I N the great and univerfal concern of religion, both fexes,
and all ranks, are equally interefted. The truly catholic fpirit
of Chriftianity accommodates itfelf, with an aftonifhing con-
defcenfion, to the circumftances of the whole human race.

L E T no miftaken girl fancy fhe gives a proof of her wit,
by her want of piety; or that a contempt of things ferious and
facred, will exalt her underftanding, or raife her character,
even in the opinion of the moft avowed male infidels.

C I C E R O fpoke it as the higheft commendation of Cato's
character, that he embraced philofophy, not for the fake of
difputing like a philofopher, but of living like one. The chief
purpofe of Chriftian knowledge, is to promote the great end
of a Chriftian life.

From the book of wifdom :—Hearken unto thy father—defpife
not thy mother when fhe is old. Extract :

  'T I S wifdom fpeaks—her voice divine
Attend my fon, and life is thine.
Thine, taught to fhun the devious way,
Where folly leads the blind aftray :
Let virtue's lamp thy footfteps guide,
And fhun the dang'rous heights of pride ;
The peaceful vale, the golden mean,
The path of life purfue ferene.
   From infancy what fufferings fpring—
While yet a naked helplefs thing,

Tho

Who o'er thy limbs a cov'ring caſt,
To ſhield thee from th' inclement blaſt?
Thy mother—honour her—her arms
Secur'd thee from a thouſand harms;
When helpleſs, hanging on her breaſt,
She ſooth'd thy ſobbing heart to reſt;
For thee her peace, her health deſtroy'd,
For thee, her ev'ry pow'r employ'd:
Thoughtful of thee, before the day
Shot thro' the dark its riſing ray;
Thoughtful of thee, when ſable night
Again had quench'd the beams of light;
To Heav'n, in ceaſeleſs pray'r for thee
She rais'd her head, and bent her knee.
Deſpiſe her not, now feeble grown—
Oh! make her wants and woes thy own;
Let not thy lips rebel; nor eyes,
Her weakneſs, frailty, years, deſpiſe;
From youthful inſolence defend,
Be patron, huſband, guardian, friend.
Thus ſhalt thou ſoothe, in life's decline,
The mis'ries that may once be thine.

A N unwary moment may happen to the moſt guarded and reſerved; and this reflection ought to fill us with charity for others.

. A PRUDENT man hath his eyes open, and his mouth ſhut; and as much deſires to inform himſelf, as to inſtruct others.

I N diſcourſe, make not too great a profuſion or expence of your knowledge, leſt your treaſure be ſoon exhauſted.

T H E thought of immortality, the hope of endleſs happineſs, is enough to animate the ſoul with the nobleſt ambition, and yet make it look, with the humbleſt compaſſion, upon that part of the creation, that wants ſo divine a hope.

The

The latter Part of the 3d Chap. of Habbakuk imitated.

ALTHO' the blooming plants forget to fhoot,
The fig-tree fade, and vines deny their fruit ;
No tafteful olives finifh our repaft,
Nor op'ning buds furvive the wintry blaft ;
The barren fields their wonted blades withhold,
And lambs no longer fill the fcanty fold ;
Nor flocks, nor herds, around the vale be feen,
But one ftern famine fweep th' impov'rifh'd green—
Yet fhall the God of nature claim my praife,
Wake my firft fongs, and fhare my lateft lays.
Each night and morn fhall ftring the duteous lyre,
And all my nerves retouch with facred fire ;
Hills, vales, and groves, the founding anthem own,
And the fweet echoes reach th' unfhaken throne,
Where reigns forever, in unclouded day,
My guide, that leads at once and lights my way.
He from my paths will turn th' oppofing wind,
And give my feet the fwiftnefs of the hind ;
Life's rugged tracts make like the pleafant plains,
On whofe fmooth ground the trav'ler fooths his pains.

"IF thine enemy hunger, feed him ; if he thirft, give him drink." That is, if we behold our enemy labouring under any extraordinary diftrefs or calamity, which it is in our power to remove, or alleviate, as in the cafe of extreme poverty, ficknefs, or misfortune, we ought then cheerfully to lend him our help and affiftance, to extricate him out of his difficulties or afflictions. An amiable example of which our Saviour affords us in the parable of the good Samaritan, who had a much better reafon for neglecting the diftreffed traveller, than either the prieft, or the Levite, viz. Becaufe he was a Jew, and therefore his declared enemy. But in him all party-animofities were overpowered by the tender feelings of pity and compaffion.

SELFISHNESS may indifferently happen to be a motive to an action, that, in itfelf, is either good or evil, either
hurtful

hurtful or beneficent. But, as far as selfishness, merely, is a motive to any action, it never had, nor can have, any relation to virtue. We must search somewhat deeper for the root of that tree, which is productive of this divine fruit.

ALL who would please the great, must be flatterers; but the true province of friendship is, to put us in mind of our own faults.

MEEKNESS makes any condition tolerable and easy to be endured. He that meekly bears any suffering, takes off the edge of it, that it cannot wound him; whereas he that frets and rages at it, whets it, and makes it much sharper than it would otherwise be.

IT is said of our blessed Saviour, that "he was led as a sheep to the slaughter; that when he was reviled, reviled not again; when he suffered, threatened not." And if he, the Lord of glory, suffered thus meekly and unjustly from his own creatures, with what face can we ever complain of any injury done to us?

BE very watchful over thine heart, and never suffer it to feed on the fancy of thy own worth; but whenever any such thought arises, beat it down immediately, with the remembrance of some of thy follies or sins, and so make this very motion of pride an occasion of humility.

NEVER compare thyself with those thou thinkest more foolish or more wicked, that so thou mayest, like the Pharisee, extol thyself for being better; but if thou wilt compare, do it with the wise and godly; and then thou wilt find thou comest so far short, as may help to pull down thy high esteem of thyself.

POVERTY is apt to betray a man into envy, riches into arrogance; poverty is too often attended with fraud, vicious compliance, repining, murmur and discontent. Riches expose a man to pride and luxury, a foolish elation of heart, and too great a fondness for the present world. In short, the middle condition is most eligible. N 2 WINTER

WINTER.

THE fields, difconfolate and fad,
   No vegetation bring ;
No verdure makes the peafant glad,
   Nor fhews the welcome fpring.
No more the trees, in lively green,
   Their leafy honours fhew ;
The boughs, where trembling leaves were feen,
   Exhibit flakes of fnow.
The plumy race of various dies,
   Have loft their wonted fire ;
To thickets clofe, from low'ring fkies,
   The feather'd tribe retire.
The chryftal floods, in fetters bound,
   No rufhing torrents feel ;
In vain, aufpicious gales are found,
   To waft the gloffy keel.
In icy fetters they remain,
   Depriv'd of liberty,
'Till gentle zephyrs loofe the chain,
   And fet the captives free.

The TRULY GREAT.

THEY'RE only great, whom no bafe motive rules,
Who owe no glory to the breath of fools ;
Friends to true merit, to their country dear,
To others kind, but to themfelves fevere ;
Quiet in fuff'ring, with their lot content,
And careful to improve the talent lent ;
Good, without pride, tho' humble, yet not mean,
In danger fearlefs, and in death' ferene.

IF every perfon would confider, that he is in this life
nothing more than a paffenger, and that he is not to fet up
his reft here, but to keep an attentive eye upon that ftate
of being to which he approaches every moment, and which
                                will

will be forever fixed and permanent; this single consideration would be sufficient to extinguish the bitterness of hatred, the thirst of avarice, and the cruelty of ambition.

I T is a great presumption, to ascribe our successes to our own management, and not to esteem ourselves upon any blessing, rather as it is the bounty of Heaven, than the acquisition of our own prudence.

⋄⟡⟡⟡⟡⟡⟡⋄

Extract from " A Midnight Thought."

W H I L E active thought unseals my eye,
And midnight darkness shades the sky,
Be hush'd, my soul, ye moments stay,
While I rejudge the guilty day.
See conscience glares, more dreadful made
By silence and the awful shade!
She points her poignard to my breast,
And bids my justice speak the rest.
Then think, my soul, while Heav'n gives breath,
And antedate the stroke of death!
Reflect how swift the moments fly,
Nor linger, unprepar'd to die!
Pensive revolve, 'ere yet too late,
The scenes of an eternal state;
A series of unnumber'd years
Or crown'd with joys, or lost in tears.
What awful hints these thoughts inspire,
They chill the blood, they pall desire;
They teach the soul her Heav'nly birth,
And banish all the pomps on earth.
Here, as in air, a bubble tost,
Her worth unknown, her genius lost;
At pleasure's fancy has she drove,
Forgetful of her seat above!
Oh! what such folly can atone?
Reason dejected from her throne;
Let humble penitence restore,
And bid my soul to err no more.

All

All clement thou, oh God! all juſt,
The good man's rock, the ſinner's truſt;
Accept the blood my Saviour ſhed,
To ſave from woe this guilty head.
Oh! ſend thy life-reſtoring grace,
Effuſe the luſtre of thy face;
From guilt and ſorrow ſet me free,
And guide me, till I come to thee.

NOTHING will give a greater luſtre to all your virtues, than modeſty.

HE that is his own appraiſer, will be miſtaken in the value.

A LITTLE eſteem of one's lelf, hinders a great deal from others; boaſting may gain applauſe from fools, but it puts a wiſe man to the expence of a bluſh.

SELF eſteem, is commonly puniſhed by univerſal contempt.

NO revenge is more heroic, than that which torments envy by doing good.

IT is in vain for him to pretend to love either God or man who loves his money ſo much better, that he will ſee his poor brother (who is a man, and bears the image of God) ſuffer all extremities, rather than part with any thing to relieve him. "He that giveth to the poor, lendeth unto the Lord"— and that too on ſolemn promiſe of repayment. "That which he hath given, will he pay him again." It is, amongſt men, thought a great diſparagement, when we refuſe to truſt them: It ſhews we either think them not ſufficient, or not honeſt. How great an affront is it then to God, thus to diſtruſt him?
Innumerable accidents there are, which may, in an inſtant, bring a rich man to beggary: And therefore, what courſe ſo prudent can we take for our wealth, as to put it out of the reach of thoſe accidents, by lending it to God, where we may be ſure to find it ready at our greateſt need, and that too with improvement and increaſe?

The

The contented Country Maid.

W H A T happinefs the rural maid attends,
In chearful labour while each day fhe fpends;
She gratefully receives what Heaven has fent,
And, rich in poverty, enjoys content.
She feldom feels the fpleen's imagin'd pains,
Nor melancholy ftagnates in her veins;
She rarely lofes life in thoughtlefs eafe,
Nor on the velvet couch invites difeafe.
Her homefpun drefs in fimple neatnefs lies,
And for no glaring equipage fhe fighs.
Her reputation, which is all her boaft,
In a malicious vifit ne'er was loft.
No midnight mafquerade her beauty wears,
And health, not paint, the fading bloom repairs.
If love and quiet in her bofom reign,
And like enjoyment in her happy fwain,
No homebred jars her quiet ftate controul,
Nor watchful jealoufy torments her foul.
With fecret joy fhe fees her little race
Reft on her knee, and her fmall cottage grace;
The fleecy ball their bufy fingers cull,
Or from the fpindle draw the length'ning wool;
Thus flow her hours, with conftant peace of mind,
Till age the lateft thread of life unwind.

O F all thofe forrows that attend mankind,
With patience bear the lot to thee affign'd,
Nor think it chance, nor murmur at the load,
For know what man calls fortune, is from God.

AMONG the antient Romans, it was not the houfe which
honoured the mafter, but the mafter the houfe. A cottage
with them became as auguft as a temple, when juftice, generofity, probity, fincerity, and honour, were lodged in it; and
how can a houfe be called fmall, which contains fo many
and fuch great virtues?

AN

A N extraordinary merit may lie hid under a mean habit, as a rich garment may cover enormous vices.

T H E nobility arising from birth, is by far inferior to that which proceeds from merit.

M A R C U S Aurelius was averse to every thing that had the air of pomp and luxury. He lay upon the bare ground ; at twelve years old he took the habit of a Philosopher ; he forbore the use of guards, the imperial ornaments, and the ensigns of honour, which were carried before the Cæsars and the Augusti. Nor was this conduct owing to his ignorance of what was grand and beautiful, but to the juster and purer taste he had of both, and to an intimate persuasion, that the greatest glory, and principal duty of man, especially if in power, and eminently conspicuous, is so far to imitate the Deity, as to throw himself into a condition of wanting as little as may be for himself, and doing all the good to others he is capable of.

I F it shews a greatness of soul to overlook our own nobility, and not suffer it to gain the ascendant over our actions, we may likewise observe, that it is no less great in such as have raised themselves by merit, not to forget the meanness of their extraction, nor be ashamed of it.

W E read in the scriptures, that Boaz, in the midst of riches, was laborious, diligent in husbandry, plain without luxury, delicacy, sloth or pride. How affable, how obliging and kind to his servants ! " The Lord be with you," says he to his reapers; and they answered him, " the Lord bless thee." This was the beautiful language of religious antiquity ; but how little known in our days.

How commendable was his behaviour towards Ruth, when he desires her not to go into any other field to glean, but to abide fast by his maidens, to eat and drink with them, and the charitable order he gives his reapers to let her glean even among the sheaves, and to let fall some of the handfuls on purpose for her that she might gather them up without being ashamed ; teaching us by this wise conduct, to save those we oblige, the confusion of receiving, and ourselves the temptation of vain-glory in giving. T H E

THE Providence of God is univerſal; it preſides over all to the minuteſt particular, and governs and directs all.

- -◇- ⬥⬥⬥⬥⬥ -◇- -

Part of the Book of Job verſified.

FOND man, the viſion of a moment made—
Dream of a dream, and ſhadow of a ſhade;
What worlds haſt thou produc'd, what creatures fram'd?
What inſects cheriſh'd, that thy God is blam'd?
When pain'd with hunger, the wild raven's brood
Call upon God, importunate for food,
Who hears their cry? Who grants their hoarſe requeſt,
And ſtills the clamour of the craving neſt?
Who taught the hawk to find, in ſeaſons wiſe,
Perpetual ſummers and a change of ſkies?
When clouds deform the year, ſhe mounts the wind,
Shoots to the ſouth, nor fears the ſtorm behind.
The ſun returning, ſhe returns again,
Lives in his beams, and leaves ill days to men.
Am I a debtor? Haſt thou ever heard
Whence come the gifts that are on me confer'd?
My laviſh fruit a thouſand vallies fills,
And mine the herds that graze a thouſand hills.
Earth, ſea and air, all nature is my own,
And ſtars and ſun are duſt beneath my throne,
And dar'ſt thou, with the world's great father vie,
Thou who doſt tremble at my creatures eye?
    Then the Chaldean eas'd his lab'ring breaſt,
With full conviction of his crime oppreſt.
Thou canſt accompliſh all things, Lord of might!
And every thought is naked to thy ſight—
But oh! thy ways are wonderful, and lie
Beyond the deepeſt reach of mortal eye.
Oft have I heard of thine Almighty pow'r,
But never ſaw thee till this dreadful hour.
O'erwhelm'd with ſhame, the Lord of life I ſee,
Abhor myſelf, and give my ſoul to thee.
Nor ſhall my weakneſs tempt thine anger more,
Man was not made to queſtion, but adore.

To

To a Child of a Month old.

BLESS'D babe, who ftranger to all worldly ftrife,
Art lately launch'd upon the fea of life;
And midft thofe dang'rous waves wilt foon be toft,
Where fome by pleafure, fome by pain, are loft—
Who yet not feels, nor fear'ft to feel the rage
Of ftorms, that threaten man's maturer age;
But view'ft, with carelefs and indiff'rent eyes,
The clouds of folly that arround thee rife.
Accept, nor fear infection from my fong,
Few authors flatter at an age fo young.
Look round the habitable world and fee,
Who would not wifh to change their place with thee.
Would not the mifer broach each fav'rite mine,
His heart as eafy, thoughts as free as thine?
What would the hoary villain not endure,
His hands as innocent, his foul as pure.
Would not the fpendthrift beg his fquander'd ore,
To purchafe half the blifs thou haft in ftore?
Ne'er was a maxim truer fure than this,
That want of innocence is want of blifs;
'Tis this, 'tis innocence, thy bofom cheers,
This calms thy troubles, this difpels thy fears;
This fpreads o'er all its beautifying rays,
Makes every object, every play-thing, pleafe.
This (whilft lefs things the guilty breaft can awe)
Gives mufick to a key, and beauty to a ftraw.
So thro' the prifm, to philofophic eyes,
The barren lawns in pleafing profpect rife.
Steep hills in azure tempt the diftant fight,
Wafte wilds look lovely in a borrow'd light.
Deck'd by the glafs the cottage apes the throne,
And fhines in colours that were ne'er its own.
Long may this pleafing calm remain within,
Unknown to trouble, as unknown to fin;
When infant reafon fhall begin to rife,
Prate on thy lips, and wanton in thy eyes,
Oh! may this charm thy ev'ry care beguile,
Affift thy prattle, and improve thy fmile.

When

When growing fenfe, to rip'ring judgment join'd,
Shall fix a doubtful empire in thy mind—
If heat of blood with wanton frenzy warm—
If eafe fhould tempt thee, or if pleafure charm,
Oh ! may this love of virtue, love of truth,
Lead thee ftill fafe thro' all the paths of youth.
Next when thy part in life's ftill varying plan
Shall call thee forward on the ftage of man,
Oh ! may it keep thee honeft, gen'rous, juft,
'True to thy word, and cautious of thy truft ;
Light in thy foul devotion's facred flame,
Make virtue all thy wifh, and Heav'n thy aim.
And laft, when manhood's vigour fhall decay,
Time fhake thy head, and filver't o'er with grey,
Long may this fov'reign remedy remain,
To prop thy weaknefs, and affuage thy pain ;
'Till the laft moment fhed its kindly ray,
And glad the ev'ning of thy well-fpent day.
But may ten thoufand pleafures rife between
Thy op'ning curtain, and this clofing fcene ;
May health attend thee, beautiful and gay,
And fmooth, thro' life, thy elfe too rugged way.

PROSPERITY quickens, and gives a fort of falfe courage to men of low, degenerate minds, and dreffes them up
in an outward grandeur, which impofes upon the majority of
mankind ; but adverfity is the touchftone of fouls truly great
and generous.

SILENCE is fometimes more fignificant and fublime,
than the moft noble and moft expreffive eloquence, and is, on
many occafions, the indication of a great mind.
But filence never fhows itfelf to fo great an advantage,
as when it is made the reply to calumny and defamation, provided that we give no juft occafion for them.

HOW different is the view of paft life, in the man who is
grown old in knowledge and wifdom, from that of him who

O   is

is grown old in ignorance and folly. The latter is like the owner of a barren country, that fills his eye with the prospect of naked hills and plains, which produce nothing either profitable or ornamental; the other beholds a beautiful and spacious landscape, divided into delightful gardens, green meadows, fruitful fields, and can scarce cast his eye on a single spot of his possessions, that is not covered with some beautiful plant or flower.

TO look upon the soul as going on from strength to strength, to consider that she is to shine forever with new accessions of glory, and brighten to all eternity; that she will be still adding virtue to virtue, and knowledge to knowledge, carries in it something wonderfully agreeable to that ambition, which is natural to the mind of man. Nay, it must be a prospect pleasing to God himself, to see his creation forever beautifying in his eyes, and drawing nearer to him, by greater degrees of resemblance.

THAT we might not want inducements to engage us in such an exercise of the body, as is proper for its welfare, it is so ordered, that nothing valuable can be procured without it. Not to mention riches and honour, even food and raiment are not to be come at without the toil of the hands, and sweat of the brows. Providence furnishes materials, but expects that we should work them up ourselves.

As for those who are not obliged to labour, by the condition in which they are born, they are more miserable than the rest of mankind, unless they indulge themselves in that voluntary labour, which goes by the name of exercise.

Thoughts on the Grave of a Child.—By a Father.

HÆRE, here she lies! oh! could I once more view
Those dear remains; take one more fond adieu;
Weep o'er that face of innocence, or save
One darling feature, from the noisome grave!
Vain wish!—now low in earth that form of love
Decays, unseen, yet not forgot above.

In

In angel light array'd, beyond the ftars,
Some more exalted form her fpirit wears.
The work of God, that beauteous clay, which here
In infant charms fo lovely could appear;
As tho' in nature's nicest model caft,
Exactly polifh'd, wrought too fine to laft—
By the fame pow'rful hand again fhall rife,
To bloom more gay, more lovely in the fkies.
No ficknefs there can the pure frame annoy,
Nor death prefume God's image to deftroy.
Thofe feats of pleafure, not a tear fhall ftain,
In them not ev'n a wifh fhall glow in vain.

That active mind, intent on trifles here,
Enlarges now to objects worth its care;
Looks down with fcorn upon the toys below,
And burns, with tranfport, better worlds to know,
Where fcenes of glory open to her fight,
And new improvements furnifh new delight;
Where friendly angels, for her guidance giv'n,
Lead her, admiring, thro' the courts of Heav'n.

No wonder then her courfe fo fwiftly run,
Like the young eaglet, tow'ring to the fun;
Wing'd for eternal blifs, and plum'd for day,
Her foul, enraptur'd, made fuch hafte away,
Impatient to regain its native fhore,
Juft fmil'd at folly, and look'd back no more.

That winning nature, and obliging mién;
Pleas'd to fee all, by all with pleafure feen.
Smiling and fweet as vernal flow'rs new blown,
Affociates now with tempers like her own.

Her love to me (how artlefs and fincere!)
Rifes from earth to Heav'n, and centers there.
So pure a flame, Heav'n's gracious Sire will own,
And with paternal love indulgent crown.

Ceafe, then, frail nature, to lament in vain,
Reafon forbids to wifh her back again;
Rather congratulate her happier fate,
And new advancement to a better ftate;
This blefling quick recall'd, can Heav'n beftow,
No more in pity to a father's woe?

Know

Know the fame God, who gave, hath tak'n away,
He orders her to go, and thee to ftay.
'Tho' in this vale of mifery, alone,
Deferted, weary, thou fhould'ft travel on,
Still be refign'd, my foul ! his will be done.

Efcap'd from life, and all its train of ills,
Which, a's ! too fure, the hoary pilgrim feels,
To fhorter trial doom'd, and lighter toil,
Ere fin could tempt her, or the world defile.
She, favour'd innocent, retires to reft,
Taftes but the cup of forrow, and is bleft.

Such the mild Saviour to his arms receives,
And the full bleffings of his kingdom gives.
'There angels wait, fubmiffive, round his throne,
'To praife his goodnefs in thefe infants fhewn.
Amidft that gentle throng, how Heav'nly bright,
Diftinguifh'd Lucy fhines, fair ftar of light.
Short, yet how pleafing, was her vifit here,
She's now remov'd to grace a nobler fphere ;
There, while thy much lov'd parents mourn below,
Thou, happy child, fhall not our forrows know.
Eternal joys be thine, full anthems raife,
And glad all Heav'n with thy Creator's praife.

IF we are firmly refolved to live up to the dictates of reafon, without any regard to wealth, reputation, or the like con-
fiderations, any more than as they fall in with our principal
defign, we may go through life with fteadinefs and pleafure ;
but if we act by feveral broken views, and will not only be
virtuous, but wealthy, popular, and every thing that has a value
fet upon it by the world, we fhall live and die in mifery and
repentance.

ENQUIRIES after happinefs, and rules for attaining it,
are not fo neceffary and ufeful to mankind, as the arts of con-
folation, and fupporting one's felf under affliction. The utmoft
we can hope for, in this world, is contentment ; if we aim at
any thing higher, we fhall meet with nothing but grief and
                                                    difappoint-

difappointments. A man fhould direct all his ftudies and endeavours, at making himfelf eafy now, and happy hereafter.

IT is of the laft importance to feafon the paffions of a child
with devotion, which feldom dies in a mind that has received
an early tincture of it. 'Tho' it may feem extinguifhed for a
while by the cares of the world, the heats of youth, or the allurements of vice, it generally breaks out, and difcovers itfelf
again as foon as difcretion, confideration, age, or misfortunes,
have brought the man to himfelf. The fire may be covered
and overlaid, but cannot be entirely quenched and fmothered.

PURE devotion opens the mind to great conceptions, and
fills it with more fublime ideas, than any that are to be met
with in the moft exalted feience ; and at the fame time warms
and agitates the foul more than fenfual pleafure.

IT is of unfpeakable advantage to poffefs our minds with
an habitual good intention, and to aim all our thoughts,
words and actions, at the fame laudable end, the glory of our
Maker, the good of mankind, and the benefit of our own fouls.

SOCRATES, on the day of his execution, a little before the draught of poifon was brought to him, entertaining
his friends with a difcourfe on the immortality of the foul, has
thefe words : " Whether or no God will approve of my actions,
I know not ; but this I am fure of, that I have at all times
made it my endeavour to pleafe him ; and I have a good hope,
that this my endeavour will be accepted by him."

HYMN.

WHEN rifing from the bed of death,
  O'erwhelm'd with guilt and fear,
I fee my Maker, face to face,
  O how fhall I appear ?
If yet, while pardon may be found,
  And mercy may be fought,

My

My heart with inward horror fhrinks,
  And trembles at the thought.
When thou, O Lord! fhalt ftand difclos'd,
  In Majefty fevere,
And fit in judgment on my foul,
  Oh! how fhall I appear?
But thou haft told the troubled mind,
  Who does her fins lament,
The timely tribute of her tears,
  Shall endlefs woe prevent.
Then fee the forrows of my heart,
  Ere yet it be too late,
And hear my Saviour's dying groans,
  To give thofe forrows weight.
For never fhall my foul defpair,
  Her pardon to procure,
Who knows thine only Son has dy'd,
  To make her pardon fure.

SELF-LOVE but ferves the virtuous mind to wake,
As the fmall pebble ftirs the peaceful lake,
The centre mov'd, a circle ftrait fucceeds,
Another ftill, and ftill another fpreads;
Friend, parent, neighbour, firft it will embrace,
His country next, and next all human race.
Wide and more wide, th' o'erflowings of the mind
Take every creature in of every kind.
Earth fmiles around with boundlefs bounty bleft,
And Heav'n beholds its image in his breaft.

IT may be laid down as a pofition, which will feldom deceive, that when a man cannot bear his own company, there is fomething wrong. He muft fly from himfelf, either becaufe he feels a tediousnefs in life from the equipoife of an empty mind, which, having no tendency to one motion, more than another, but as it is impelled by fome external power, muft always have recourfe to foreign objects; or he muft be afraid of the intrusion of fome unpleasing ideas, and is, perhaps,

haps, ſtruggling to eſcape from the remembrance of a loſs, the fear of a calamity, or ſome other thought of greater horror.

C A N a mortal look down, without giddineſs and ſtupe-faction, into the vaſt abyſs of eternal wiſdom? Can a mind, that ſees not infinitely, perfectly comprehend any thing among an infinity of objects mutually relative? Remember, that per-fect happineſs cannot be conferred on a creature, for perfect happineſs is an attribute as incommunicable, as perfect power and eternity.

Extract from Cowper's Poem called the Taſk.

——————————DETESTED ſport!
That owes its pleaſures to another's pains ;
That feeds upon the ſobs and dying ſhrieks
Of harmleſs nature ; dumb, but yet endued
With eloquence, that agonies inſpire,
Of ſilent tears and heart diſtending ſighs.
Vain tears, alas ! and ſighs that ſeldom find
A correſponding tone in jovial ſouls.
Well, one at leaſt is ſafe ; one ſhelter'd hare
Has never heard the ſanguinary yell
Of cruel man exulting in her woes.
Innocent part'ner of my peaceful home,
Whom ten long year's experience of my care
Has made at laſt familiar, ſhe has loſt
Much of her vigilant, inſtinctive dread,
Not needful here beneath a roof like mine.
Yes, thou may'ſt eat thy bread, and lick the hand
That feeds thee ; thou may'ſt frolic on the floor
At ev'ning, and at night retire ſecure
To thy ſtraw couch, and ſlumber unalarm'd,
For I have gain'd thy confidence, and pledg'd
All that is human in me, to protect
Thine unſuſpecting gratitude and love.
If I ſurvive thee, I will dig thy grave,
And when I place thee in it, ſighing ſay;
I knew at leaſt one hare that had a friend.

CRUEL

CRUEL sports, were thought very high reflections on the politeness of the Romans. Are they not much greater on the mercy and humanity of Christians?

IT behoves us to accustom ourselves to a sober, modest way of speaking, and to avoid all those modes of speech, which border upon, or naturally lead to falshood.

BE careful to practise nothing which you are ashamed of; to do nothing for which you need be afraid of the eye or ear of God, and the world, then will you be under no temptation of lying, to conceal what you have done amiss.

IF we had true notions of God, and eternity, right notions of ourselves, and of the world, they could not fail to create in us thoughts full of humility towards ourselves, full of contempt towards the vain world, full of the highest adoration towards God, and full of earnestness to acquire a happy eternity.

PRAYER, unaccompanied with a fervent love of God, is like a lamp unlighted; the words of the one, without love, being as unprofitable as the oil and cotton of the other, without flame.

HE alone is a great man, whose heart is strongly disposed to acts of humanity and benevolence; and who has fortitude enough to do his duty in all circumstances of life; who acts for the good of mankind, as long as he is able, and then finishes his course in the cause of virtue.

THE way to avoid prejudice, is to govern the passions with a steady hand; to treat all things, in a calm and disinterested manner, not suffering our desires or aversions to be moved, but by a just consideration of real usefulness.

TAKE but the humblest lilly of the field,
And if our pride will to our reason yield,
It must by sure comparison be shewn,
That on the regal seat great David's son,

Array'd

Array'd in all his robes and types of pow'r,
Shines with lefs glory, than that fimple flow'r.

   ENOUGH I think my prefent ftore
Nor do I afk of Heav'n for more,
But thank the kindnefs of my God,
For that fmall ftock he has allow'd.
Lo time ftill waftes, and waftes away,
And moons arife but to decay ;
Then why, fond mortals, tell me why!
Ye raife your coftly domes fo high ?
Why build ye palaces fo great,
With all th' extravagance of ftate,
When ev'ry ftone muft fall away,
And crumble ftill, and ftill decay ?
Why ftrive ye to enrich ye more,
With ware from every foreign fhore,
When death ftands knocking at your door ?

PRAYER.

THERE is fuch a thing as converfe with God in prayer,
and it is the life and pleafure of a pious foul ; without it we are
no Chriftians, and he that practifes it moft, is the beft follower
of Chrift ; for our Lord fpent much time in converfe with his
Heavenly Father. This is balm that eafes the moft raging
pains of the mind, when the wounded confcience comes to the
mercy-feat, and finds pardon and peace there. This is the cordial that revives and exalts our natures, when the fpirit, broken with forrows, and almoft fainting to death, draws near
to the Almighty phyfician, and is healed and refrefhed.

THE mercy-feat in Heaven is our fureft and fweeteft refuge
in every hour of diftrefs and darknefs upon earth ; this is our
daily fupport and relief, while we are paffing through a world
of temptations and hardfhips, in the way to the promifed land.
" It is good to draw near to God."

THE

THE Creator is to be firſt loved for his own ſake, for his infinite goodneſs and perfection, and then the creature, as his work, and in proportion to its reſemblance to him.

HE that thinks twice before he ſpeaks once, will ſpeak twice the better for it.

⸻⊷⊶◇⊶⊷⊷⊷⊷⊷⊶◇⊶⸻

WHEN in thy ſacred preſence, Lord ! I bow,
Let true devotion in my boſom glow ;
There, with the ſenſe of thy great goodneſs fraught,
May I with care correct each wand'ring thought ;
Drink at my ears the preacher's Heav'nly lore,
And ſtill the more I hear, improve the more ;
Make this ſhort life an earneſt of the next,
And all my acts a comment on thy text.

On the Vanity of Riches.

SEEST thou, fond youth, yon precipice on high,
Rob'd by the clouds, and turban'd by the ſky,
How low'ring darkly o'er the ſhadow'd plains,
It ſtrikes wild terror thro' the gazing ſwains ?
Its craggy ſides can boaſt no fertile ſoil,
No promis'd harveſt tempts a rural toil ;
No grazing cattle find their paſture there,
Nor fragrant flowers perfume the ambient air ;
No ſweet-meand'ring current glides along,
Courting the meadows with its murm'ring ſong ;
No ſhady bow'rs adorn its barren ſides,
Nor fair encloſure its rough ground divides ;
No lofty ſpires a wond'ring glance invite,
Nor artful gardens tempt the diſtant ſight.
All rough and wild, it rears its rocky head,
And ſtrikes the wond'ring eye with awful dread.
From its high top impetuous torrents flow,
Form'd by diſſolving tracts of native ſnow ;
Sorrow ſits brooding on its furrow'd face,
And deſolation triumphs o'er the place.

Seeſt

Seeſt thou all this, fond mortal ? Think, if ſo,
Thou ſeeſt the bliſs the vain ambitious know.
Such are the barren pleaſures they enjoy,
For this alone whole ages they employ.
They move our pity, tho' they tempt our ſight,
High above all, but wretched by their height.

···◇···◈◆◈◆◈◆◈◆◈···◇···

THE prince of peace—He firſt reconciled God to man,
and then endeavoured to reconcile men to each other. When he
came into the world, he, by his angels, proclaimed peace ; and
when he left the world, he bequeathed the ſame as his legacy :
" Peace I leave with you," &c.

THE merciful man will extend his hand of relief and comfort, as far as he may, to his fellow-creatures, whether they
labour under temporal or ſpiritual diſtreſs, whether they call
for his pity from their ſins or from their ſorrows ; while, in
every relation of life, he will exerciſe this Heavenly temper :
As a magiſtrate, gentle and humane, however compelled, in
certain caſes, to be ſeverely juſt : As a creditor, mild and forbearing, not flying haſtily and vigorouſly to the utmoſt extremity, much leſs condemning the unhappy debtor to im-
priſonment, which may utterly incapacitate from all power and
hope of payment ; and in ſhort, in every caſe exerciſing that
lenity, mildneſs, forgiveneſs, and mercy, whereof the eternal
God hath ſet us ſo bright an example ; and all our expectation
of which from him, he hath made to depend on our ſhewing
the ſame to others : " Bleſſed are the merciful, for they ſhall
obtain mercy."

···◆◈◆◈◆◈◆◈◆◈···

——————————YE good diſtreſs'd,
Ye noble few !—who here unbending ſtand
Beneath life's preſſure, yet bear up a while,
And what your bounded view, which only ſaw
A little part, deem'd evil, is no more ;
The ſtorms of wintry time will quickly paſs,
And one unbounded ſpring encircle all. On

- On the Nativity of Chrift.

A W A K E from filence every voice,
   Each chearful pipe and founding ftring ;
Let ev'ry grateful heart rejoice,
` And ev'ry tongue in rapture fing.
On this diftinguifh'd day of grace
   Th' eternal Prince of glory came,
To purge the guilt of human race,
   And fave them by his pow'rful name.
Bow down your heads, ye lofty pines,
   Ye mountains crown'd with cedars tall ;
Be ftill, ye rude, imperious winds,
   Throughout the wide terreftrial ball.
Let nought but harmony and love
   O'er all th' expanded furface reign,
And let the facred choir above
   Approve, and join the Heav'nly ftrain.
When we in bondage were exil'd,
   And rebels to th' eternal God,
Our fouls, with blackeft guilt defil'd,
   Obnoxious to th' impending rod ;
That from his feat of perfect blifs
   The Son of glory fhou'd defcend,
To offer man the terms of peace,
   And his unbounded grace extend.
Such goodnefs, fuch ftupendous grace !
   Nor men, nor angels can explore ;
Then let us, what we cannot trace,
   With awful reverence adore.
Ye wing'd inhabitants of air,
   All ye that graze the verdant plain ;
Ye herds, that to the wilds repair,
   And ye that fkim the furging main,
Some figns of exultation fhow,
   While grateful minds your voices raife,
'Tis all that mortals can below,
   To hail the day in fongs of praife.
While fkilful hands the chorus join,
   And tune the rapture-raifing lyre, `

While grateful ftrains of love divine,
   Serene, extatic joys infpire.
Thus facred be the happy day,
   While fun, and moon, and ftars endure;
Till nature feels her laft decay,
   And time itfelf fhall be no more.

LET us entertain a general good opinion of all men, till unqueftionable evidence fhall oblige us to give up that good opinion ; yet, at the fame time, let us be cautious not to fuffer our good opinion to betray us into any improper compliances or connexions.

SELL not your hopes of Heavenly treafures, nor any thing that belongs to your eternal intereft, for any of the advantages of the prefent life : " What fhall it profit a man, to gain the whole world, and lofe his own foul ?"

TO piety join modefty and docility, reverence of your parents, and fubmiffion to thofe who are your fuperiors in knowledge, in ftation, and in years. Dependence and obedience belong to youth. Modefty is one of its chief ornaments ; and has ever been efteemed a prefage of rifing merit.

PROVIDENCE never intended, that any ftate here fhould be either completely happy, or entirely miferable. If the feelings of pleafure are more numerous, and more lively, in the higher departments of life, fuch alfo are thofe of pain. If greatnefs flatters our vanity, it multiplies our dangers. If opulence encreafes our gratifications, it encreafes, in the fame proportion, our defires and demands. If the poor are confined to a more narrow circle, yet, within that circle, lie moft of thofe natural fatisfactions, which, after all the refinements of art, are found to be the moft genuine and true.

WE have feen, that inordinate paffions are the great difturbers of life ; and that, unlefs we poffefs a good confcience, and a well governed mind, difcontent will blaft every enjoyment,

P   and

and the higheſt proſperity will prove only diſguiſed miſery. Fix then this concluſion in your mind, that the deſtruction of your virtue, is the deſtruction of your peace. "For our rejoicing is this, the teſtimony of our conſcience, that in ſimplicity, and godly ſincerity, not with fleſhly wiſdom, but by the grace of God, we have had our converſation in the world, and more abundantly to you-wards." 2 Cor. i. 12.

Caution againſt Pride.

CONSIDER what you ſhall be. Your fleſh returns to corruption and common earth again ; nor ſhall your duſt be diſtinguiſhed from the meaneſt beggar or ſlave ; no, nor from the duſt of brutes and inſects, or the moſt contemptible of creatures ; and as for your ſouls, they muſt ſtand before God, in the world of ſpirits, on a level with the reſt of mankind, and diveſted of all your haughty and flattering circumſtances. None of your vain diſtinctions in this life, ſhall attend you to the judgment-ſeat. Keep this tribunal in view, and pride will wither, and hang down its head.

MONEY, like manure, does no good, till it is ſpread ; there is no real uſe of riches, except in the diſtribution ; the reſt is all conceit.

BY love directed, and in mercy meant,
Are trials ſuffer'd, and afflictions ſent.
To ſtem impetuous paſſion's furious tide ;
To curb the inſolence of proſp'rous pride ;
To wean from earth, and bid our wiſhes ſoar
To that bleſt clime, where pain ſhall be no more,
Where wearied virtue ſhall for refuge fly,
And every tear be wip'd from ev'ry eye.

HAPPY are they who preſerve their innocence unſullied by any great or wilful crimes, and who have only the common failings of humanity to repent of ; theſe are ſufficiently mortifying to a heart deeply ſmitten with the love of virtue, and with the deſire of perfection. "WHAT-

"WHATSOEVER ye would that men fhould do un-
to you, even fo do unto them." There is no occafion, great
or fmall, on which you may not fafely apply this rule for the
direction of your conduct; and, whilft your heart honeftly ad-
heres to it, you can never be guilty of any fort of injuftice or
unkindnefs.

ENDEAVOUR to acquire a temper of univerfal candour and benevolence; and learn neither to defpife nor condemn any perfons on account of their particular modes of faith
and worfhip; remembering, always, that goodnefs is confined
to no party—that there are wife and worthy men among all
the fects of Chriftians—and that to his own mafter, every one
muft ftand or fall.

VIRTUE is the foundation of honour and efteem, and
the fource of all beauty, order, and happinefs, in nature.

BEAUTY and wit will die, learning will vanifh away,
and all the arts of life be foon forgot; but virtue will remain
forever.

A GOOD word is an eafy obligation; but not to fpeak
ill, requires only our filence, which cofts us nothing.

The FIRE-SIDE.

I.

DEAR Chloe, while the bufy crowd,
The vain, the wealthy, and the proud,
    In folly's maze advance:
Tho' fingularity and pride
Be call'd our choice, we'll ftep afide,
    Nor join the giddy dance.

II.

From the gay world we'll oft retire,
To our own family and fire,
    Where love our hours employs:

No noisy neighbours enter here,
No intermeddling stranger near,
  To spoil our heart-felt joys.

III.

If solid happiness we prize,
Within our breasts this jewel lies ;
  And they are fools who roam :
The world has nothing to bestow,
From our own selves our joys must flow,
  And that dear hut our home.

IV.

Of rest was Noah's dove bereft,
When, with impatient wing, she left
  That safe retreat, the ark :
Giving her vain excursion o'er,
The disappointed bird once more
  Explor'd the sacred bark.

V.

Tho' fools spurn Hymen's gentle pow'rs,
We who improve his golden hours,
  By sweet experience know,
That marriage, rightly understood,
Gives to the tender, and the good,
  A paradise below.

VI.

Our babes shall richest comforts bring ;
If tutor'd right, they'll prove a spring
  Whence pleasures ever rise :
We'll form their minds with studious care,
To all that's manly, good and fair,
  And train them for the skies.

VII.

While they our wisest hours engage,
They'll joy our youth, support our age,
  And crown our hoary hairs :
They'll grow in virtue every day,
And thus our fondest loves repay,
  And recompence our cares.

VIII.

No borrow'd joys, they're all our own,
While to the world we live unknown,
   Or by the world forgot ;
Monarchs ! we envy not your ftate ;
We look with pity on the great,
   And blefs our humble lot.

IX.

Our portion is not large indeed,
But then how little do we need,
   For nature's calls are few :
In this the art of living lies,
To want no more than may fuffice,
   And make that little do.

X.

We'll, therefore, relifh with content,
Whate'er kind Providence has fent,
   Nor aim beyond our pow'r :
For if our ftock be very fmall,
'Tis prudence to enjoy it all,
   Nor lofe the prefent hour.

XI.

To be refign'd when ills betide,
Patient when favours are deny'd,
   And pleas'd with favours giv'n :
Dear Chloe, this is wifdom's part,
This is that incenfe of the heart,
   Whofe fragrance fmells to Heav'n !

XII.

We'll afk no long, protracted treat,
(Since winter-life is feldom fweet)
   But when our feaft is o'er,
Grateful from table we'll arife,
Nor grudge our fons, with envious eyes
   The relics of our ftore.

XIII.

Thus hand in hand, thro' life we'll go,
Its chequer'd paths of joy and woe
   With cautious fteps we'll tread :

Quit

Quit its vain scenes without a tear,
Without a trouble, or a fear,
   And mingle with the dead.

XIV.

While conscience, like a faithful friend,
Shall through the gloomy vale attend,
   And cheer our dying breath :
Shall, when all other comforts cease,
Like a kind angel whisper peace,
   And smooth the bed of death !

    SINCERITY is firm and substantial, and there is nothing hollow or unsound in it ; and because it is plain and open, fears no discovery ; of which the crafty man is always in danger.

    PLUTARCH has written an essay on the benefits which a man may receive from his enemies ; and mentions this in particular, " that, by the reproaches cast upon us, we see the worst side of ourselves, and open our eyes to several blemishes and defects in our lives and conversations, which we should not have observed without the help of such ill-natured monitors."

    LET us " keep the heart with all diligence, seeing out of it are the issues of life." Let us account our mind the most important province which is committed to our care ; and as we cannot rule events, study at least to rule ourselves.

    It is common with the young, even when they resolve to tread the path of virtue and honour, to set out with presumptuous confidence in themselves. Trusting to their own abilities, for carrying them successfully through life, they are careless of applying to God, or of deriving any assistance from what they are apt to reckon the gloomy discipline of religion. Alas ! how little do they know the dangers which await them ?"
    Neither human wisdom, nor human virtue, unsupported by religion, are equal for the trying situations which
                    often

often occur in life. By the fhock of temptation, how frequently have the moft virtuous intentions been overthrown !
Under the preffure of difafter, how often has the greateft conftancy funk ! Deftitute of the favour of God, you are in no better fituation, with all your boafted abilities, than orphans left
to wander in a tracklefs defart, without any guide to conduct
them, or any fhelter to cover them from the gathering ftorm.
Correct, then, this ill-founded arrogance. Expect not that
your happinefs can be independent of him who made you. By
faith and repentance, apply to the Redeemer of the world.
By piety and prayer, feek the protection of the God of Heaven.

THE cheerfulnefs of a well-regulated mind, fprings from
a good confcience, and the favour of Heaven, and is bounded
by temperance and reafon. It makes a man happy in himfelf,
and promotes the happinefs of all around him. It is the clear
and calm funfhine of a mind illuminated by piety and virtue.
It crowns all other good difpofitions, and comprehends the general effect which they ought to produce on the heart.

LET no man rafhly determine, that his unwillingnefs to
be pleafed, is a proof of underftanding, unlefs his fuperiority
appears from a lefs doubtful evidence; for though peevifhnefs
may fometimes boaft its defcent from learning or from wit,
it is much oftener of bafe extraction, the child of vanity and
nurfling of ignorance.

LET the virtuous remember, amidft all their fufferings,
that though the heart of the good man may bleed, even to
death, he will never feel a torment equal to the rendings of
remorfe.

PLATO being told, that he had many enemies who fpake
ill of him, " It is no matter, faid he, I will live fo that none
fhall believe them." Hearing, at another time, that an intimate friend of his had fpoken detractingly of him, " I am fure
he would not do it, fays he, if he had not fome reafon for it."
This is the fureft, as well as the nobleft way, of drawing the
fting out of a reproach, and the true method of preparing a

man

man for that great and only relief againſt the pains of calumny, a good conſcience.

JUDGE not of mankind in general from the conduct of a few individuals. There are perſons capable of alleviating all our cares by a friendly participation, and of heightening every ſatisfaction by ſharing them. Cultivate an acquaintance with the truly deſerving, and the painful remembrance of ingratitude will ſoon be loſt in the reciprocal endearments of ſincere friendſhip.

DOST thou aſk a torch to diſcover the brightneſs of the morning? Doſt thou appeal to argument for proofs of divine perfection? Look down to the earth on which thou ſtandeſt, and lift up thine eye to the worlds that roll above thee : Thou beholdeſt ſplendour, abundance and beauty; is not he who produced them mighty? Thou conſidereſt—is not he who formed thy underſtanding, wiſe? Thou enjoyeſt—is not he who gratifies thy ſenſes, good? Can aught have limited his bounty, but his wiſdom? or can any defects be therein diſcovered by thy ſagacity?

RELIGION preſcribes to every miſerable man, the means of bettering his condition; it ſhews him, that the bearing of his afflictions as he ought to do, will naturally end in the removal of them; it makes him eaſy here, becauſe it can make him happy hereafter.

A CONTENTED mind is the greateſt bleſſing a man can enjoy in this world ; and if in the preſent life his happineſs ariſes from the ſubduing of his deſires, it will ariſe in the next from the gratification of them.

EVERY wiſe man will conſider this life only as it may conduce to the happineſs of the other, and cheerfully ſacrifice the pleaſures of a few years to thoſe of an eternity.

HOWEVER far ſome men may have gone in the ſcience of impartiality, perhaps there is not one of them but would be ſurprized, if he could be ſhewn how much farther he might go.

T H O'.

T H O' poor the peafant's hut, his feafts tho' fmall,
He fees his little lot, the lot of all ;
Sees no contiguous palace rear its head,
To fhame the meannefs of his humble fhed ;
No coftly lords the fumptuous banquet deal,
To make him loathe his vegetable meal—
But calm, and bred in ignorance and toil,
Each wifh contracting, fits him to the foil ;
Cheerful at morn he wakes from fhort repofe,
Breathes the keen air, and carrols as he goes ;
With patient angle trolls the finny deep,
Or drives his vent'rous plough-fhare to the fteep ;
Or feeks the den, where fnow-tracks mark the way,
And drags the ftruggling favage into day.
At night returning, every labour fped,
He fits him down, the monarch of a fhed ;
Smiles by his cheerful fire, and round furveys
His childrens looks, that brighten at the blaze ;
While his lov'd partner, boaftful of her hoard,
Difplays the cleanly platter on the board.

E V E R Y ftation of life has duties, which are proper to it.
Thofe who are determined, by choice, to any particular kind
of bufinefs, are indeed more happy than thofe who are determined by neceffity ; but both are under an equal obligation of
fixing on employments, which may be either ufeful to themfelves, or beneficial to others.

N O one of the fons of Adam, ought to think himfelf exempt from that labour and induftry, which were denounced
upon our firft parent, and in him, to all his pofterity. Thofe
to whom birth or affluence may feem to make fuch an application unneceffary, ought to find out fome calling or profef-
fion for themfelves, that they may not lie as a burden on the
fpecies, and be the only ufelefs parts of the creation.

I T fometimes happens, that too clofe an attention to minute
exactnefs, or a too rigorous examination of every thing, by
the

the standard of perfection, vitiates the temper, rather than improves the understanding, and teaches the mind to discern faults with unhappy penetration. It is incident, likewise, to men of vigorous imaginations, to please themselves too much with futurities, and to fret, because those expectations are disappointed, which should never have been formed.

KNOWLEDGE and genius are often enemies to quiet, by suggesting ideas of excellence, to which men, and the performances of men, cannot attain.

WE should always act with great cautiousness and circumspection, in points where it is not impossible that we may be deceived.

— ⦿⦿⦿⦿ —

LET no fond love of earth exact a sigh,
　　No doubt divert our steady steps aside,
Nor let us long to live, or dread to die,
　　Heav'n is our hope, and Providence our guide.

A Thought on waking.

SLEEP by night, and cares by day,
Bear my fleeting life away :
Lo in yonder eastern skies,
Sol appears, and bids me rise,
Tells me, "life is on the wing,
And has no returning spring :
Death comes on with steady pace
And life's the only day of grace."
Shining preacher ! happy morning !
Let me take th' important warning ;
Rouse then all my active pow'rs,
Well improve the coming hours ;
Let no trifles kill the day,
(Trifles oft our hearts betray.)
Virtue, science, knowledge, truth,
Guide th' enquiries of my youth.
Wisdom, and experience sage,

Then

Then shall soothe the cares of age ;
Those with time shall never die,
Those will lead to joys on high ;
Those the path of life display,
Shining with celestial day ;
Blissful path ! with safety trod,
As it leads the soul to God.

ON HAPPINESS

LONG have I sought the wish of all,
  True happiness to find,
Which some will wealth, some pleasure call,
  And some a virtuous mind.
Sufficient wealth, to keep away
  Of want the doleful scene,
And joy enough to gild the day,
  And make life's course serene.
Virtue enough to ask my heart,
  Art thou secure within ?
Hast thou perform'd an honest part ?
  Hast thou no private sin ?
This to perform, these things possess,
  Must raise a noble joy,
Must constitute that happiness,
  Which nothing can destroy.

  O ! THOU, whose pow'r o'er moving worlds presides,
Whose voice created, and whose wisdom guides,
On darkling man, with fond effulgence shine,
And cheer the clouded mind with light divine.
'Tis thine alone to calm the pious breast,
With silent confidence and holy rest,
From thee, great God ! we spring, to thee we tend,
Path, motive, guide, original and end.

--◇--◁◇◁◇◁◇◁◇◁◇--◇--

IT was a common saying among the Heathens, that the
wise man hates nobody, but only loves the virtuous. The
Christian owes a more general love.

A

A Thought on Death.

DEATH, to a good man, is but paffing through a dark entry, out of one little dufky room of his father's houfe, into another, that is fair and large, lightfome, glorious and divinely entertaining.

THERE is nothing of greater importance to us, than to fift our thoughts, and examine all the dark receffes of the mind, if we would eftablifh our fouls in fuch a folid and fubftantial virtue, as will turn to account in that great day, when it muft ftand the teft of infinite wifdom and juftice.

ALL the real pleafures and conveniences of life, lie in a narrow compafs; but it is the humour of mankind, to be always looking forward, and ftraining after thofe who have got the ftart of them in wealth and honour.

A Good confcience is to the foul, what health is to the body; it preferves a conftant eafe and ferenity within us, and more than countervails all the calamities and afflictions which can poffibly befal us. I know nothing fo hard for a generous mind to get over, as calumny and reproach; and cannot find any method of quieting the foul under them, befides this fingle one, of our being confcious to ourfelves, that we do not deferve them.

The Rural Scene.

SWEET contemplation to purfue,
Behold a rural fcene in view,
The bleating herds, the lowing kine,
The fpreading oak, the tow'ring pine;
The air, from noxious vapours free,
Whilft fquirrels trip from tree to tree,
And the fweet fongfters hover round,
Fruit, herbs and flow'rs, enrich the ground,
And each their various fruits produce,
Some for delight, and fome for ufe.

Behold,

Behold, O! youth, this scene, and see
What nature's God hath given to thee.
With wonder view his great designs,
In which superior wisdom shines ;
Revere his name, admire his love,
And raise thy thoughts to' worlds above.

·--◆--◎◎◎◎◎◎◎◎--◆--·

To the Poor.

T H E Providence of Almighty God, has placed you under difficult circumstances of life, and daily reads you a lesson in a more particular manner to depend upon him. This you may be assured of for your comfort, that you are under God's constant and immediate care : And one advantage you enjoy above the rich, in your journey to Heaven, is, that you are not clogged and hindered in your course thither, by those manifold incumbrances which lie on them ; of whom our Saviour hath said, " That it is very hard for them to enter into the kingdom of Heaven." Their temptations are proportioned to their abundance ; their cares are more and their distractions greater ; so that you have no reason to envy them, nor repine at your own condition ; and these are chiefly your temptations, and against these you must be more particularly watchful. Certainly, if you consider things aright, you will find that your store-house is the most sure, your supply most certain ; for you are immediately in the hands of God, of him who feedeth the ravens, and cloatheth the grass of the field ; so that you may be much more assured that he will cloathe you. Endeavour to be humble, holy, Heavenly minded ; always remembering, that he is the poorest man, who is poor in grace. Your Saviour had not where to lay his head ; let his example serve to reconcile your low condition to you ; and let your religious behaviour under it, be the means to sanctify it.

W H E R E V E R we turn our eyes, we find something to revive our curiosity, and engage our attention. In the dusk of the morning, we watch the rising of the sun, and see the day diversify the clouds, and open new prospects in its gradual

Q   advance.

advance. After a few hours, we see the shades lengthen, and the light decline, till the sky is resigned to a multitude of shining orbs, different from each other in magnitude and splendour. The earth varies its appearance, as we move upon it; the woods offer their shades, and the fields their harvests; the hill flatters with an extensive view, and the valley invites with shelter, fragrance and flowers.

LET not the curious from your bosom steal
Secrets, where prudence ought to set her seal;
Yet be so frank and plain, that at one view,
In other things, each man may see you thro'.

GOD of my soul! without thy strength'ning grace,
How weak, how poor, how blind, is human race!
To sound thy praise, ten thousand worlds agree,
And nature lifts the grateful song to thee;
To thee, with awe, the brute creation bends,
When thunder bursts, or stormy rain descends;
Obedient to thy will, the rocks and trees
Now rest in snow; now bless the vernal breeze;
Yet man, presuming on his glimm'ring sense,
Rash man alone disclaims thy Providence;
The truths he dare not controvert, denies,
And 'gainst conviction shuts his ears and eyes.

OUR follies, when display'd, ourselves affright,
Few are so bad, to bear the hideous sight;
Mankind in herds, thro' force of custom stray,
Mislead each other into error's way,
Pursue the road, forgetful of the end,
Sin by mistake, and without thought offend.

SHE who values not the virtue of modesty in her words and dress, will not be thought to set much price upon it in her actions.

IN

I N cafe of temptation, it is a prudent caution to avoid the encounter, when we are conscious of weaknefs, or unable to withftand it.

M O S T men are ready enough to reckon up the income of their eftates, and compute how it will anfwer their feveral expences ; but few employ their arithmetic to calculate the value and income of their life and time, or confider how they may be expended to the beft advantage. In thefe the beggar has as large a revenue as the king, though they are juftly accounted the more valuable treafure.

T H E foul, agitated with paffions, fares like a weak bird in a ftormy day ; fhe is not able to make a ftraight flight, but is toffed from the track fhe would purfue, being loft and carried in the air at the pleafure of the winds. In this condition is the foul, till, by a conftant meditation on God, and application to him, it has obtained a ftrong and vigorous faith to ballaft and ftrengthen it, and enable it to maintain the ftraight and fteady courfe of virtue.

S T I L L as thro' life's meandring path I ftray,
Lord ! be the fweet companion of my way ;
A kind conductor to the bleft abode
Of light, of life, of happinefs and God.

R E L I G I O N's facred lamp alone
   Unerring, points the way,
Where happinefs forever fhines
   With unpolluted ray.

Written on a Watch.

W E R E but our minds, like this machine,
Unmov'd by paffion, or by fpleen,
And, true to nature's guardian pow'r,
Could mark, with goodnefs, ev'ry hour,
Then health and joy would follow too,
As laws of thought and motion do ;
Sweet health to pafs the moments o'er,
And joy when time fhall be no more.   'T I S

'TIS a contradiction to imagine, that reputation or praise is a suitable recompence for virtue ; since it is a reward that nothing but vanity can make acceptable ; it declares a man both foolish and vicious, that can be pleased and satisfied with it; and that his merit is only owing to his pride

TRUE virtue, as it has no other aims than the service and honour of God, so the least and only recompence it aspires to, is his approbation and favour.

MY God ! my all-sufficient good !
  My portion and my choice ;
In thee are all my hopes renew'd,
  And all my powers rejoice.

GRANT me to live, and if I live, to find
The dear lov'd portion of a peaceful mind ;
That health, that sweet content, that pleasing rest
Which God alone can give, as suits me best.

CHARITY.

CHARITY, decent, modest, easy, kind,
Softens the high, and rears the abject mind ;
Knows with just reins, and gentle hand to guide,
Betwixt vile shame, and arbitrary pride.
Not soon provok'd, she easily forgives ;
And much she suffers, as she much believes ;
Soft peace she brings wherever she arrives,
She builds our quiet, as she forms our lives ;
Lays the rough paths of peevish nature ev'n,
And opens in each heart a little Heav'n.

THERE is no preservative from vice, equal to an habitual and constant intercourse with God : Neither does any thing equally alleviate distress, or heighten prosperity ; in distress it sustains us with hope, and in prosperity it adds to every other enjoyment, the delight of gratitude.   IN

I N true good nature, there is neither the acrimony of spleen nor the sullenness of malice; it is neither clamorous nor fretful, neither easy to be offended, nor impatient to revenge; it is a tender sensibility, a participation of the pains and pleasures of others, and is, therefore, a forcible and constant motive, to communicate happiness, and alleviate misery.

I T should be a general rule, never to utter any thing in conversation, which would justly dishonour us if it should be reported to the world.

T O a benevolent disposition, every state of life will afford some opportunities of contributing to the welfare of mankind. Opulence and splendour are enabled to dispel the cloud of adversity, to dry up the tears of the widow and the orphan, and to encrease the felicity of all around them. Their example will animate virtue, and retard the progress of vice. And even indigence and obscurity, tho' without power to confer happiness, may at least prevent misery, and apprize those who are blinded by their passions, that they are on the brink of irremediable calamity.

O REPUTATION! dearer far than life,
Thou precious balsam, lovely sweet of smell,
Whose cordial drops once spilt by some rash hand,
Not all thy owner's care, nor the repenting toil
Of the rude spoiler, ever can collect
To its first purity and native sweetness.

Solomon's good Wife paraphrased.   Proverbs, 31st Chapter.

T H E wife, in whose soft, faithful bosom, dwells
    The mingled warmth of love and virtue's flame,
As much in worth the ruby's price excells,
    As greatest merits highest honours claim.
On her the partner of her breast relies,
    In her can fullest confidence repose,
Can ev'n the pride and spoils of war despise,

For

For good, not ill, from all her conduct flows.
The wool and flax employ her willing hands,
    And tho' domestic arts are most her care,
Yet, as the merchant-ship from distant lands
    Brings precious freight, she brings her food from far.
E'er light she forces sleep's soft bands to yield,
    And to her houshold gives refreshment due ;
With careful earnings purchases a field,
    And, still more wond'rous, plants a vineyard too.
By daily use her arms their strength encrease—
    Her merchandize is good, she gladly finds ;
And as by day her labours rarely cease,
    By night her candle unextinguish'd shines.
Her lib'ral hand extends to all the poor,
    Bestowing alms as diff'rent wants require ;
Nor fears her houshold hardships may endure,
    For they in scarlet boast a rich attire.
To cloathe herself she weaves gay tapestry,
    Purple and silk the labour of her hand,
With which bedeck'd, her husband sits on high,
    Distinguish'd 'midst the elders of the land.
Fine linen, also, by her art is made,
    And girdles offer'd to the merchant's choice,
While she in strength and honour well array'd,
    Thro' times to come shall happily rejoice.
The law of kindness in her heart presides,
    The words of wisdom from her lips distil,
A meek discretion thro' her houshold guides,
    And duteous all their destin'd task fulfil.
Her children, rising up with grateful voice,
    Pronounce her blest, as love or prudence sways,
Her husband, conscious of his happy choice,
    With pleasure joins their voluntary praise.
Tho' many wives, in this and ages past,
    Of virtuous conduct bright examples shine,
Yet all to her, the first as well as last,
    The palm of female excellence resign.
True as when spoke, remains the royal word,
    " That favour's transient, and all beauty vain ;"
But she who keeps his law, and fears the Lord,
    Shall the just tribute of applause obtain.   WHEN

WHEN we confider the different allotments of Providence to his creature man, in this ftate of exiftence, and compare the wants and fufferings of fome, with the eafe and affluence of others, we fhould be almoft ready to conclude, that the prefcrving care of our Heavenly Father, was not equally extended to all; though he has affured us in fcripture, that he is no refpecter of perfons; but we muft be very cautious of making fuch an inference; for as our Great Creator fees not as we fee, and has a view in all his difpenfations to the ultimate good of his creatures, we ought rather to fuppofe, that the particular condition of every man, fo far from being an impeachment of divine impartiality, is alloted him in perfect wifdom, in order to his happinefs at laft.

THE neceffities of the poor may be intended as the moft certain means of preferving their health, and keeping them moral, temperate and humble, which are great virtues. While the fuperfluities of the rich, by fubjecting them to many vices, may render the final account of their ftewardfhip a matter of the greateft anxiety and diftrefs of mind, to which no temporal fuffering can be equivalent. Hence, if we confider prefent lefs grievous than future evil, it will appear, in this comparative view of the higher and lower ranks of men, that the difference is rather in favour of the latter, under all the preffures and mortifications of poverty.—Yet this is by no means to be ufed as an argument by the opulent, for withholding affiftance and fupport from their fellow-creatures, in real want of them; for humanity, and, the cardinal virtue, charity, call upon and require all, who are able, to fuccour and relieve fuch objects— to which may be added, that this is a duty particularly enjoined by our bleffed Saviour, who has told us, as a forcible incitement to the practice of it, that fuch as give to the poor, lend to the Lord, which is telling us, in other words, that by this means treafure is to be laid up in Heaven.

SIMPLICITY, the infeparable companion both of geniune grace, and of real modefty, if it doth not always ftrike at firft (of which it feldom fails) is fure, however, when it does ftrike, to produce the deepeft and moft permanent impreffions.

IN

IN folitude I'll fpend the day;
The fultry hour I'll pafs away,
 In calm retirement's feat;
Enraptur'd, fnatch her peaceful joys,
While others court ambition's toys,
 And ftudy to be great.

THE BEGGAR.

"PITY the forrows of a poor old man,
 Whofe trembling limbs have led him to your door;
Whofe days are dwindled to the fhorteft fpan,
 Oh! give relief, and Heav'n fhall blefs your ftore.
Thefe tatter'd rags my poverty befpeak,
 Thefe hoary locks proclaim my length of years,
And many a furrow, in my grief-worn cheek,
 Has been the channel to a ftream of tears.
Yon houfe erected on the rifing ground,
 With tempting afpect drew me from the road,
For plenty, there a refidence has found,
 And grandeur, a magnificent abode.
Hard is the cafe of the infirm and poor,
 There begging for a morfel of their bread,
A pamper'd menial thruft me from the door,
 To feek a fhelter in an humbler fhed.
Oh! take me to your hofpitable dome,
 Keen blows the wind, and piercing is the cold,
Short is my paffage to the friendly tomb,
 For I am miferably poor and old.
Heav'n fends afflictions—why fhould we repine?
 Here happinefs we ne'er were born to fee,
Too foon, alas! your lot may be like mine,
 The child of forrow and of mifery.
Was I to tell the fource of every grief,
 If foft compaffion ever touch'd your breaft,
Your hand could not withhold the kind relief,
 And tears of pity could not be repreft.
A little farm was my paternal lot,
 Then, like the lark, I fprightly hail'd the morn,
But ah! oppreffion drove me from my cot,

My cattle dy'd, and blighted was my corn.
My daughter, once the comfort of my age,
   Lur'd by a villain, left her native home,
Is now abandon'd on the world's wide ftage,
   And doom'd in fcanty poverty to roam.
My tender wife, fweet foother of my care,
   With anguifh felt the fore calamity,
Fell, ling'ring fell, a victim to defpair,
   And left the world, and wretchednefs, to me.
Pity the forrows of a poor old man,
   Whofe trembling limbs have led him to your door,
Whofe days are dwindled to the fhorteft fpan,
   Oh! give relief, and Heav'n will blefs your ftore."

EVERY thing, overdone, is liable to fufpicion. Innocence, in women, wants not the aid of oftentation; like integrity in men, it refts in its own confcioufnefs.

AS cheerfulnefs is the moft natural effect of real goodnefs, it is alfo its moft powerful recommendation. Wifdom is never fo attractive, as when fhe fmiles.

SHE that cannot " weep with them that weep," as well as rejoice with them that rejoice," is a ftranger to one of the fweeteft fources of enjoyment, no lefs than to one of the nobleft leffons of Chriftianity. Thofe are the happieft difpofitions, which are the beft.

THERE is not any thing more contemptible, or more to be pitied, than that turn of mind, which, finding no entertainment in itfelf, none at home, none in books, none in rational converfation, nor in the intercourfes of real friendfhip, nor in ingenious works of any kind, is continually feeking to ftifle reflection in a tumult of pleafures, and to divert wearinefs in a crowd.

FEMALE modefty is often filent; female decorum is never bold. Both forbid a young woman to lead the conver-
                               fation;

fation ; and true religion dreads every thing that might look
oftentatious. The moft prudent courfe you can purfue, is to
affociate, as much as poffible, with thofe that from real principle love the fhade.

I F thou wouldeft bear thy neighbour's faults, caft thine eye
upon thine own.

T H E truly humble man, fuffers quietly, and patiently, internal troubles ; and he is the man that makes great way in a
little time, like one that fails before the wind.

P E R F E C T I O N does not confift in teaching the truth,
but in doing it, becaufe he is neither the greateft faint, nor the
wifeft man, that knows the truth moft, but he that practifes it.

W H E N a young woman behaves to her parents in a manner particularly tender and refpectful, from principle as well as
nature, their is nothing good or gentle, that may not be expected from her, in whatever condition fhe is placed.

The unknown World—On hearing a Paffing Bell.

HARK, my gay friend, that folemn toll
Speaks the departure of a foul.
'Tis gone—that's all we know, not where,
Or how th' unbody'd foul does fare.
In that myfterious world none knows,
But God alone to whom it goes ;
To whom departed fouls return
To take their doom, to fmile or mourn.
Oh ! by what glimm'ring light we view,
The unknown world we're haft'ning to.
Swift flies the foul—perhaps 'tis gone
A thoufand leagues beyond the fun ;
Or twice ten thoufand more thrice told,
Ere the forfaken clay is cold.
And yet who knows, if friends we lov'd,

Tho'

Tho' dead, may be so far remov'd, *Thu dea my be So far*
Only this vail of flesh between,
Perhaps they watch us, tho' unseen.
Whilst we their loss lamenting say,
They're out of hearing far away,
Guardians to us, perhaps they're near,
Conceal'd in vehicles of air,
And yet no notices they give,
Nor tell us how or where they live.
Tho' conscious, while with us below,
How much themselves desir'd to know,
As if bound up by solemn fate,
To keep this secret of their state ;
To tell their joys or pains to none,
That man might live by faith alone.
Well, let my Sov'reign, if he please,
Lock up his marvellous decrees ;
Why should I wish him to reveal
What he thinks proper to conceal ?
It is enough that I believe
Heav'n's brighter than I can conceive ;
And he that makes it all his care
To serve God here, shall see him there.
But oh ! what worlds shall I survey,
The moment that I leave this clay ;
How sudden the surprize—how new—
Let it, my God ! be happy too !

FROM the consideration of God, as he is in himself power, wisdom, goodness, beauty and felicity itself, children must be often excited and stirred up to the desire of esteeming him, of praising him, of honouring him as he deserves, and of pleasing him in every thing. They must be made to understand, that this is the principal end for which we are sent into the world, namely, to esteem, honour and praise God, without ceasing, by the continual desires and elevations of our hearts to him ; and that, since this is the employment of angels, by being exercised in it, we become their companions in this
world,

world, and even fellow-citizens of Heaven with them, by imitating those divine spirits.

SINCE both the imagination and the memory, are faculties which have the most strength, and most activity in children, it would be well to cultivate them from the very beginning, that we may communicate unto them as much knowledge of the things of their salvation, as is possible, and as they are capable of receiving.

SILENCE is necessary on many occasions, but you must always be sincere and courteous: You ought to retain some thoughts, but disguise none.

AND, from the prayer of want, and plaint of woe,
　O! never, never, turn away thine ear;
Forlorn, in this bleak wilderness below,
　Ah! what were man, should Heav'n refuse to hear?
To others do (the law is not severe)
　What to thyself thou wishest to be done;
Forgive thy foes, and love thy parents dear,
　And friends and native land; nor those alone,
All human weal and woe learn thou to make thine own.

TRUE dignity is his, whose tranquil mind
　Virtue has rais'd above the things below,
Who ev'ry hope and fear to Heav'n resign'd,
　Shrinks not, tho' adverse winds may keenly blow.

WE should be cautious and circumspect in all our ways, and watchful over ourselves, living in the fear of God all the day long, that we sin not against him.

LET us all endeavour to be spiritually-minded, and set our affections on things above; subdue our passions, be peaceable and loving, meek, courteous, modest, teachable and governable, not wise in our own conceit, not wilful or stubborn.

We

W E muſt be contented with our preſent condition, not murmuring or repining at it, or either ambitiouſly or covetouſly ſeeking one more high or plentiful ; neither fretting and vexing our own ſouls, nor envying others ; but leaving freely all things to God's diſpoſal, and ſubmitting cheerfully to his providence.

M A Y. we wiſely improve every talent that God has given us ; doing as much good as we can with every thing, both to ourſelves and others. We muſt ſhun ſloth and idleneſs, vain paſtimes, and ſuperfluous recreations, coſtly vanities, unprofitable ſtudies and employments.

I N the evening reaſon with thyſelf and ſay, how have I ſpent this day ? Am I better than I was yeſterday ? Have I overcome any vice ? and hath God's grace been effectual in me ? if it has, then let my ſoul rejoice exceedingly, and aſcribe to her Lord the glory of her good actions.

T H E heart is the fountain, and our words are the ſtreams ; and if the fountain be muddy, the ſtreams proceeding from it, cannot be clear.

B E my ambition only to excel
In the bleſt art, " the art of living well ;"
Who this attains, bids ſin and ſorrow ceaſe,
With hope looks Heav'n-ward, and ſhall die in peace.

ON A WATCH.

W H I L E this gay toy attracts thy ſight,
  Thy reaſon let it warn ;
And ſieze, my dear, that rapid   me,
  That never muſt return.
If idly loſt, no art or care
  The bleſſing can reſtore ;
And Heav'n requires a ſtrict account
  For ev'ry miſpent hour.
Short is our longeſt day of life,

R   And

And foon its profpect ends,
Yet on that day's uncertain date
Eternity depends.
Yet equal to our being's aim
The fpace to virtue giv'n ;
And ev'ry minute, well improv'd,
Secures an age in Heav'n.

Fielding

YIELDING to immoral pleafures, corrupts the mind ;
living to animal and trifling ones, debafes it ; both, in their degree, difqualify it for its genuine good, and confign it over to
wretchednefs. Whoever would be really happy, muft make
the diligent and regular exercife of his fuperior powers his chief
attention, adoring the perfections of his Maker, expreffing good
will to his fellow-creatures, and cultivating inward rectitude.

THE greateft honour you can pay to the author of your
being, is by fuch a cheerful behaviour, as difcovers a mind fatisfied with his difpenfations.

THE fcripture fays, we are to forgive until feventy times
feven ; that is, perpetually, thofe who do repent ; and thofe
who do not repent, but perfift in injuring us, we are to pray
for, and be willing to do acts of charity and humanity to
them, when need requires ; and not to revenge, but much rather to defire their amendment, and by all reafonable means
promote reconciliation.

ONE part, one little part, we dimly fcan,
  Thro' the dark medium of life's fev'rifh dream,
Yet dare arraign the whole ftupendous plan,
  If but that little part incongruous feem.—
Nor is that part perhaps what mortals deem ;
  Oft from apparent ill our bleffings rife ;
Oh ! then, renounce that impious, felf-efteem,
  For thou art but of duft ; be humble, and be wife.
                                        GOOD-

GO D-NATURE is not of less importance to our-selves than to others. The morose and petulant first feel the anguish that they give : Reproach, revilings and invective, are but the overflowings of their own infelicity, and are constantly again forced back upon their source.

The Ten Commandments.

RENOUNCE all other Gods, but only me,
And to no image bow thy heart or knee.
Take not the awful name of God in vain,
Nor e'er his holy sabbath day prophane.
Honour thy parents, and thou long shalt live,
Commit not murder, but all wrongs forgive.
From filthy lusts, keep soul and body free,
Nor steal, tho' press'd by dire necessity.
Against thy neighbour, ne'er false witness bear,
Nor covet goods, in which thou hast no share.

From Pope's Essay on Man.

LO, the poor Indian ! whose untutor'd mind
Sees God in clouds, or hears him in the wind ;
His soul proud science never taught to stray
Far as the solar walk, or milky way ;
Yet simple nature to his hope has giv'n
Behind the cloud-topt hill, an humbler Heav'n ;
Some safer world, in depth of woods embrac'd,
Some happier island in the watry waste,
Where slaves once more their native land behold,
No fiends torment, no Christians thirst for gold.
To be content's his natural desire,
He asks no angel's wing, no seraph's fire,
But thinks, admitted to that equal sky,
His faithful dog shall bear him company.

SO much have our common pursuits, which we plead as the means of supporting life, diverted men from the true ends for which they were sent into the world, that the judicious and

pious

pious, in all ages, since the time of Solomon, have readily subscribed to his opinion, that all of them are indeed "vanity and vexation of spirit." For we find there are some who spend their whole time in grammar and rhetoric, or in learning to speak well, without allowing themselves any leisure to study the more important concern of living well.

Others there are, who are so busy in finding out the riddles of a logical sphinx, that they examine all the trifles and impertinencies of reason, to find out what reason is, and in the search thereof, oftentimes lose themselves and their reason too.

There are many, who, by arithmetic, learn to divide every thing into the most minute fractions, and yet do not know how to divide an halfpenny with a poor afflicted brother in the way of charity.

Many there are, who, by the help of geometry, can set limits to grounds, and separate them from one another; can measure cities and countries, and yet cannot attain to any rule whereby they are enabled to measure themselves.

The musician can bring different voices and tones into one harmony, and yet all the while may have nothing that is harmonious in his own mind; nothing, which, by reason of its perturbation, does not run counter to all musical measures.

The astronomer, whilst with fixed eyes he looks up to Heaven, and attentively views the motion of the stars, very frequently stumbles into the next ditch; and while he is foretelling things to come, loses those that are present; for tho' with fixed eyes he looks up to Heaven, yet his mind is too much darkened and defiled with the mire of this world, to think of a better.

The philosopher disputes gravely and accurately, of the nature of things, and yet, perhaps, is no wiser than a real child, as to the nature of himself, and the things of Heaven.

The physician takes care of the health of others, but as to the knowledge of the diseases of his own mind, may be as blind as a beetle; he diligently watches the variations of his patient's pulse, but how to cure the evil dispositions, and wrong tempers, in himself, he knows and cares but little about them.

The historian has the Theban and Trojan wars at his fingers ends, but is almost wholly ignorant of a much higher concern, the proper knowledge of himself. The

The lawyer, though he has spent whole years in the construction and exposition of human laws, for the government of others, is too often but little acquainted with that divine law which teaches and enjoins a strict government over his own actions.

The theologist, earnestly contends for, and disputes about faith, but too seldom thinks of charity ; he speaks much of God, but to help his neighbour in time of need, has too little concern.

The merchant is very solicitous of gain from every port to which he can extend his trade, or in which he can obtain credit—yet seldom troubles his head in establishing a correspondence with that happy country, which offers the richest merchandize—that neither moth can corrupt, or thieves have power to steal.

The farmer, tho' daily exercised with much toil and fatigue, in breaking up and improving the most stubborn and rugged soils, with a view to a beneficial crop, yet how does he neglect, year after year, to break up and improve the barren soil of his own heart, which, without equal care and cultivation, will never produce that crop of good works, which makes truly rich, and adds no sorrow.

Arts and sciences do indeed weary the minds of men with continual labour, but yield them no true felicity.

It is religion, only, can regulate the heart—it causes it to melt in sympathy with distress, or to glow with pleasure at the happiness of another—it is that alone can harmonize the mind,
 " Attuning all its passions into peace."

The astronomer, if enlightened by it, must contemplate, with wonder and admiration, those luminaries which his eye so often gazes on with pleasure. The philosopher too, when the wonders of nature are opened to his view, with what adoration and gratitude must he look to that great source from whence they flow ! And in all professions, how imperfect is man unless illumined by the bright rays of religion, which, like the glorious luminary, the sun, will enlighten all our paths.

H Y M N

HYMN.

THE Lord my pasture shall prepare,
And feed me with a shepherd's care;
His presence shall my wants supply,
And guard me with a watchful eye;
My noon-day walks he shall attend,
And all my midnight hours defend.

2.

When in the sultry glebe I faint,
Or on the thirsty mountain pant,
To fertile vales, and dewy meads,
My weary, wand'ring steps he leads,
Where peaceful rivers, soft and flow,
Amid the verdant landskip flow.

3.

Tho' in the paths of death I tread
With gloomy horrors overspread,
My stedfast heart shall fear no ill,
For thou, O Lord! art with me still;
Thy friendly crook shall give me aid,
And guide me thro' the dreadful shade.

4.

Tho' in a bare and rugged way,
Thro' devious, lonely wilds I stray,
Thy beauty shall my pains beguile—
The barren wilderness shall smile,
With sudden greens and herbage crown'd,
And streams shall murmur all around.

NO thought is beautiful, which is not just; and no thought
can be just, which is not founded in truth.

WE are apt to fancy, that we shall be happy and satisfied,
if we possess ourselves of such and such particular enjoyments;
but either by reason of their emptiness, or the natural inquietude
of the mind, we have no sooner gained one point, but we extend our hopes to another. We still find new inviting scenes
and landscapes, lying behind those which at a distance terminated our view, IF

IF we hope for what we are not likely to poſſeſs, we act and think in vain, and make life a greater dream and ſhadow than it really is.

An Autumnal Reflection.

In fading grandeur, lo ! the trees
    Their tarniſh'd honour ſhed ;
While every leaf-compelling breeze
    Lays their dim verdure dead.
Ere' while they ſhot a vig'rous length,
    Of flow'rs, and fruit, and green ;
Now, ſhorn of beauty and of ſtrength,
    They ſtand a ſhatter'd ſcene !
Ere' long the genial breath of ſpring
    Shall all their charms renew ;
And flow'rs, and fruit, and foliage bring,
    All pleaſing to the view !
Thus round and round the ſeaſons roll,
    In one harmonious courſe,
And pour convictions on the ſoul
    With unremitting force.
Not ſuch is mans's appointed fate—
    One ſpring alone he knows !
One ſummer, one autumnal ſtate,
    One winter's dead repoſe.
Yet, not the dreary ſleep of death,
    Shall e'er his pow'rs deſtroy,
But man ſhall draw immortal breath
    In endleſs pain or joy.
Important thought !—oh mortal ! hear
    On what thy peace depends ;
The voice of truth invites thine ear,
    And this the voice ſhe ſends.
" When virtue glows with youthful charms,
    How bright the vernal ſkies !
When virtue like the ſummer warms,
    What golden harveſts riſe !"
When vices ſpring without controul,

What

What bitter fruits appear!
A wintry darknefs wraps the foul
    And horrors clofe the year.
Let youth to virtue's fhrine repair,
    And men their tribute bring,
Old age fhall lofe its load of care,
    And death fhall lofe its fting.
Borne upwards on feraphic wing,
    Their happy fouls fhall foar,
And there enjoy eternal fpring,
    Nor fear a winter more.

THERE is nothing in nature unworthy of a wife man's regard, becaufe the moft inferior of all her productions, may, in fome light or another, be made inftrumental to his improvement.

☞ THERE is fuch a clofe affinity betwen a proper cultivation of a flower garden, and a right difcipline of the mind, that it appears difficult for a rightly thoughtful perfon, that has made any proficiency in the one, to avoid paying a due attention to the other. That induftry and care which are fo requifite to cleanfe a garden from all forts of weeds, will naturally fuggeft to him how much more expedient it would be to exert the fame diligence in eradicating all forts of prejudices, follies and vices, from the mind, where they will be as fure to prevail, without a great deal of care and correction, as common weeds in a neglected piece of ground. And as it requires more pains to extirpate fome weeds than others, according as they are more firmly fixt, more numerous, or more naturalized to the foil ; fo thofe faults will be found the moft difficult to be fuppreffed, which have been of the longeft growth, and taken the deepeft root ; which are more predominate in number, and moft congenial to the conftitution.

IF our common life is not a common courfe of humility, felf-denial, renunciation of the world, poverty of fpirit, and Heavenly affection, we do not live the lives of Chriftians.

WEAK

WEAK and imperfect men, shall, notwithstanding their frailties and defects, be received, as having pleased God, if they have done their utmost to please him.

THE rewards of charity, piety and humility, will be given to those whose lives have been a careful labour to exercise these virtues in as high a degree as they could.

VALUE no man but for his probity, and living up to the rules of piety and justice. If integrity does not make you prosperous, it will at least keep you from being miserable; for no man can be truly religious, that is not likewise conscientiously just and honest.

A SOUND faith is the best divinity; a good conscience the best law; and temperance the best physic.

A Soliloquy on Death.

TO die is but to take a last farewel
Of life, and all its transitory cares;
To close our eyes and shut out day forever.
Thus much we know: And that this frail existence
Shall to its sister earth again return,
To pulverize, and be dissolv'd to nought.
To die (however awful seems the found)
Is but to lay us peaceful down to rest,
Sink into sleep, and waken in eternity.
   Whence then proceeds this coward fear of death,
These conscience-working pangs, that plague us all,
And make us sink, e'en to the grave itself,
At the bare mention? Has not that Great Cause,
The Eternal One, whose wisdom cannot err,
From the beginning of the earliest time,
Declar'd, that man and all his race, should die?
   'Tis the essential passport that must bring
(No matter when, or how, or soon, or late)
All nature to that never-ending state,
Which immortality alone can give.   The

The foul, then, as inftructed from above,
Soon as it quits its lifelefs, clay-cold corfe,
Mounts on the borrow'd filver plumes of Heav'n,
Thro' chequ'ring clouds, and foars above the ftars.
    But, oh ! who dare enquire its fate decreed ?
For Heav'n that knowledge interdicts to man,
And ftupifies the bufy, wand'ring fenfe,
That may attempt this fecret to explore.

    G R A N T I may ever, at the morning ray,
Open with pray'r the confecrated day ;
Tune thy great praife, and bid my foul arife,
And with the mounting fun afcend the fkies ;
As that advances, let my zeal improve,
And glow with ardour of confummate love ;
Nor ceafe at eve, but with the fetting fun
My endlefs worfhip fhall be ftill begun.

              Extract from young's laft Day.

    H A V E angels finn'd, and fhall not man beware?
How fhall a fon of earth decline the fnare ?
Not folded arms, and flacknefs of the mind,
Can promife for the fafety of mankind :
None are fupinely good : Thro' care and pain,
And various toils, the fteep afcent we gain.
This is the fcene of combat, not of reft,
Man's is laborious happinefs at beft ;
On this fide death his dangers never ceafe,
His joys are joys of conqueft, crown'd with peace.

www.ingramcontent.com/pod-product-compliance
Lightning Source LLC
Chambersburg PA
CBHW030832270326
41928CB00007B/1007